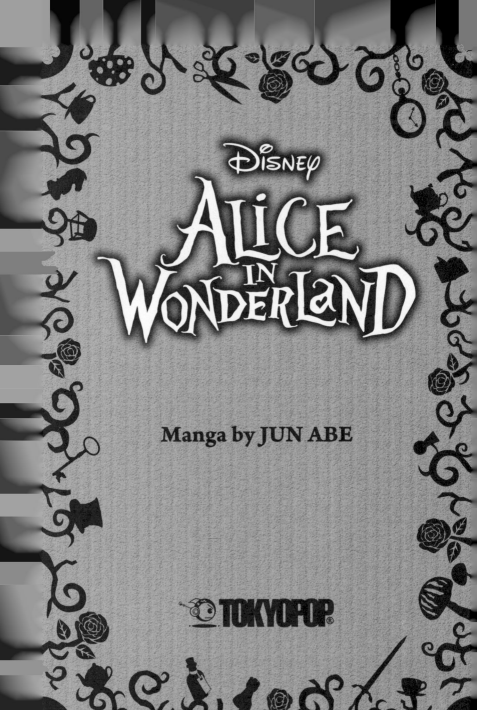

Disney ALICE IN WONDERLAND

Manga by JUN ABE

TOKYOPOP®

Alice In WonderLand

contents

Alice In WonderLand

DEAR CURIOUS READER:

WELCOME TO TOKYOPOP'S PRESENTATION OF THE *DISNEY ALICE IN WONDERLAND* MANGA, WRITTEN AND ILLUSTRATED BY JUN ABE AND ADAPTED INTO ENGLISH BY THE TOKYOPOP EDITORIAL TEAM. THIS MANGA IS INSPIRED OF COURSE BY THE DISNEY FILM BY AUTEUR TIM BURTON, WHICH IS INSPIRED OF COURSE BY THE CLASSIC LEWIS CARROLL NOVEL. HOW REMARKABLE!

OUR EXPECTATIONS ARE SUCH THAT YOU SHALL GREET THIS MANGA AND ITS SIMPLE CRY "READ ME!" BY OPENING UP ITS PAGES AND TURNING, TURNING, TURNING UNTIL YOUR HEAD SPINS AROUND AND AROUND IN WONDER. AFTER ALL, JUN ABE'S INTRICATE ILLUSTRATIVE PROWESS WOULD STOP EVEN THE SCARIEST OF SCARY BEASTS IN THEIR TRACKS.

NOW THEN, BEGIN AT THE BEGINNING, AND GO ON 'TIL YOU COME TO THE END: THEN STOP!

TOKYOPOP EDITORIAL TEAM

1 A Curious Party

LONDON, 1855
THIS VENTURE IS IMPOSSIBLE!
CHARLES, YOU HAVE FINALLY LOST YOUR SENSES.
AS LORD ASCOT SAYS, THIS IS SIMPLY TOO RECKLESS!

THE ONLY WAY TO ACHIEVE THE IMPOSSIBLE ...
THAT MAY WELL BE SO, GENTLEMEN.
...IS TO BELIEVE IT IS POSSIBLE.
I'M WILLING TO TAKE THAT CHANCE. IMAGINE TRADING POSTS IN RANGOON, BANGKOK, JAKARTA...
THAT KIND OF THINKING COULD RUIN YOU!

ALICE!
THE NIGHTMARE AGAIN?

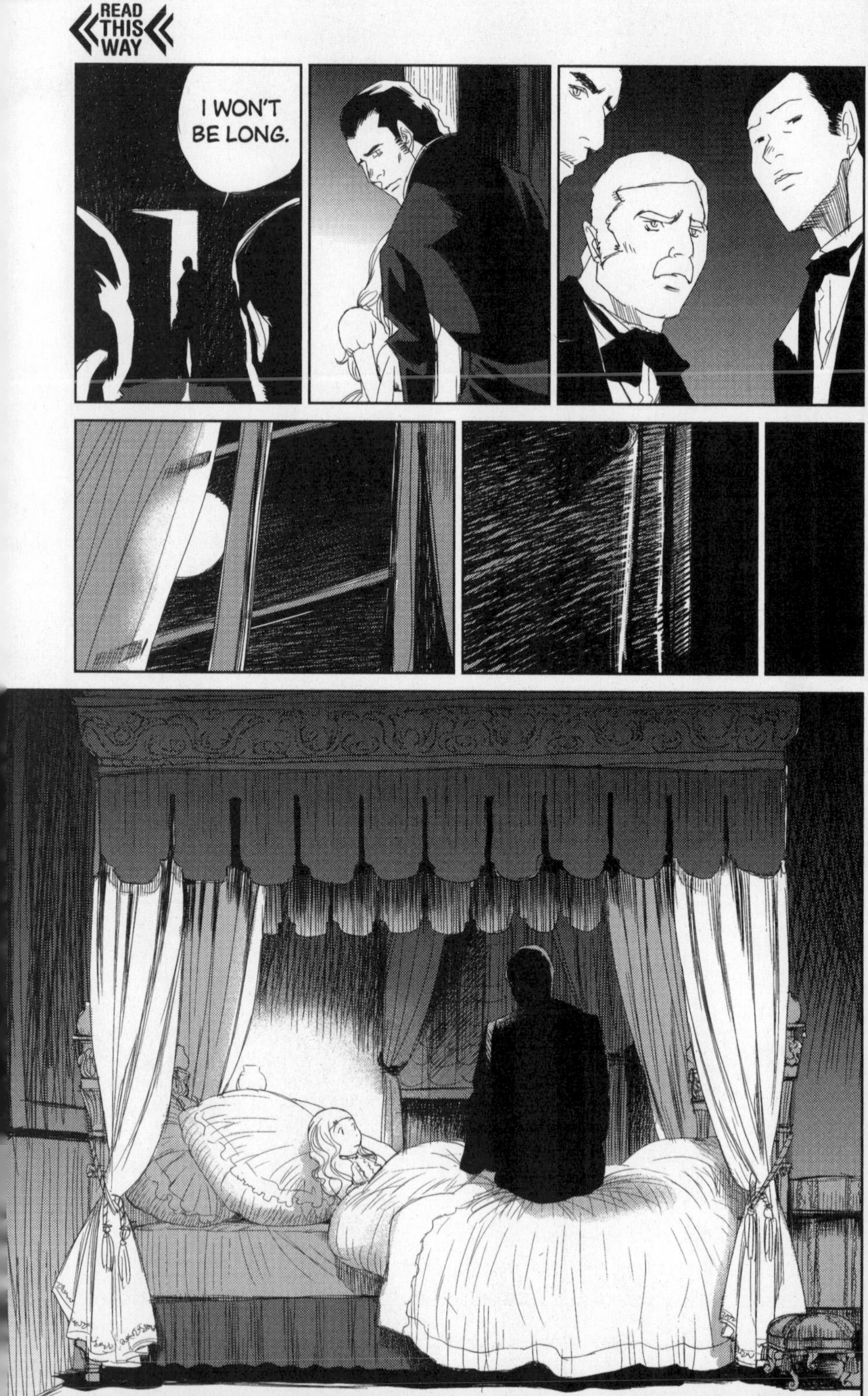
READ THIS WAY
I WON'T BE LONG.

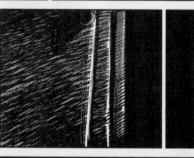

I'M FALLING DOWN A DARK HOLE, AND THEN I SEE STRANGE CREATURES...
WHAT KIND OF CREA-TURES?
WELL, THERE'S A DODO BIRD, A RABBIT IN A WAISTCOAT, A SMILING CAT...
I DIDN'T KNOW CATS COULD SMILE...
NEITHER DID I.
OH, AND THERE'S A BLUE CATER-PILLAR!

READ THIS WAY
BLUE CATER-PILLAR?
HMM...
DO YOU THINK I'VE GONE 'ROUND THE BEND?
I'M AFRAID SO. YOU'RE MAD. BONKERS.
BUT LET ME TELL YOU SOMETHING.
AND THIS IS A SECRET, YOU UNDER-STAND ...

...ALL THE BEST PEOPLE ARE.
IT'S ONLY A DREAM, ALICE. NOTHING CAN HARM YOU THERE. BUT IF YOU GET TOO FRIGHTENED, YOU CAN ALWAYS WAKE UP.
IN FACT, GIVE THIS A GO AND YOU'LL WAKE RIGHT UP!
ぷにっ
HEY!
ポカ ポカ
ポカ
OOOH... PAPA!

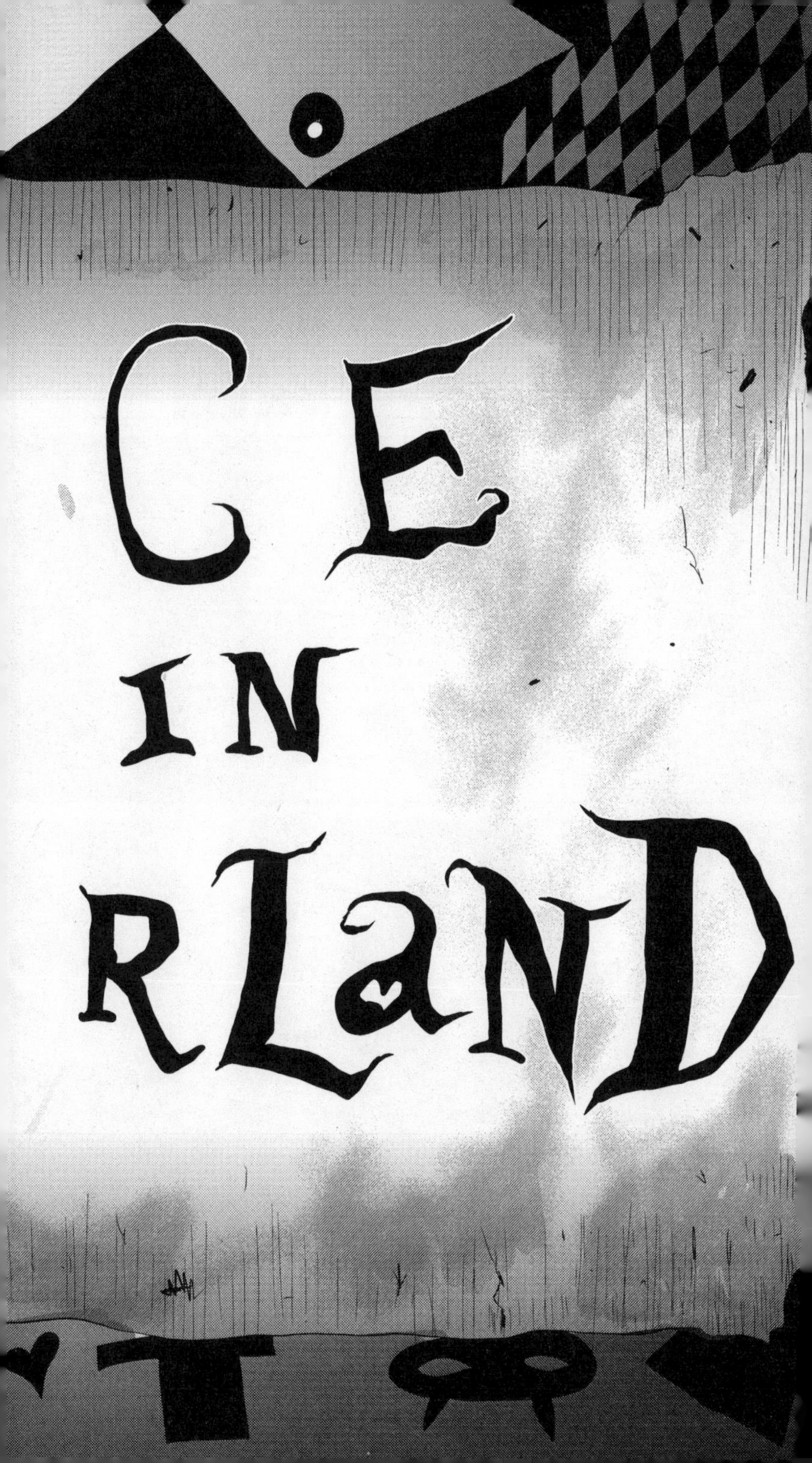
CE
IN
RLAND

ALI
WONDE

TEN YEARS LATER ...
ALICE!
OH, ALICE!
AH...
WHAT, MOTHER?
DON'T 'WHAT' ME. PAY ATTEN-TION!
MUST WE GO TO THE PARTY? I DOUBT THEY'LL NOTICE IF WE NEVER ARRIVE.
THEY WILL NOTICE!
WHERE'S YOUR CORSET?
AND NO STOCKINGS EITHER??
HEY!

WHO'S TO SAY WHAT IS PROPER?
HMPH... I'M AGAINST WEARING STOCKINGS.
"AGAINST" THEM? BUT YOU'RE NOT PROPERLY DRESSED.
ALICE!!
WHAT IF IT WAS AGREED THAT "PROPER" WAS WEARING A CODFISH ON YOUR HEAD? WOULD YOU WEAR IT?
FATHER WOULD HAVE LAUGHED.
PLEASE LISTEN TO ME, ALICE. JUST THIS ONCE.
TO ME, A CORSET IS LIKE A CODFISH.
ALICE ...
I...I'M SORRY. I MUST BE TIRED.

ONLY ONE. IT'S ALWAYS THE SAME, EVER SINCE I CAN REMEMBER. DO YOU THINK THAT'S NORMAL? DON'T MOST PEOPLE HAVE DIFFERENT DREAMS?
DID YOU HAVE BAD DREAMS AGAIN...?
I DON'T KNOW. THERE! YOU'RE BEAUTIFUL.
NOW, CAN YOU MANAGE A SMILE?

ALICE!
YOU DO REALIZE IT'S WELL PAST FOUR! NOW EVERYTHING WILL HAVE TO BE RUSHED THROUGH!
ALICE, HAMISH IS WAITING TO DANCE WITH YOU. GO!
AT LAST! WE THOUGHT YOU'D NEVER ARRIVE.
PLEASE FORGIVE MY WIFE.
NEVER MIND!
I AM SORRY. WE...

IF ONLY CHARLES WERE HERE...
MY CONDOLENCES, MADAM.
I THINK OF YOUR HUSBAND OFTEN. HE WAS TRULY A MAN OF VISION.
THANK YOU.
I HOPE YOU DON'T THINK I HAVE TAKEN ADVANTAGE OF YOUR MISFORTUNE ...
OF COURSE NOT. I'M PLEASED THAT YOU'VE PURCHASED THE COMPANY.
I WAS A FOOL FOR NOT INVESTING IN HIS MAD VENTURE WHEN I HAD THE CHANCE.
CHARLES THOUGHT SO, TOO.

TEEHEE
DO I AMUSE YOU?
HAMISH, DO YOU EVER TIRE OF THE QUADRILLE?
ON THE CONTRARY. I FIND IT INVIGO-RATING.

NO.
I HAD A SUDDEN VISION OF ALL THE LADIES IN TOP HATS AND MEN WEARING BONNETS.
IT WOULD BE BEST TO KEEP YOUR VISIONS TO YOURSELF. WHEN IN DOUBT, REMAIN SILENT.

WITHOUT PAPA AROUND, THERE'S NO ONE IN THIS WORLD WHO REALLY UNDERSTANDS ME...
PAPA...
PARDON US! MISS KINGSLEIGH IS DISTRACTED TODAY.
WHERE IS YOUR HEAD?
I WAS WONDERING WHAT IT WOULD BE LIKE TO FLY.

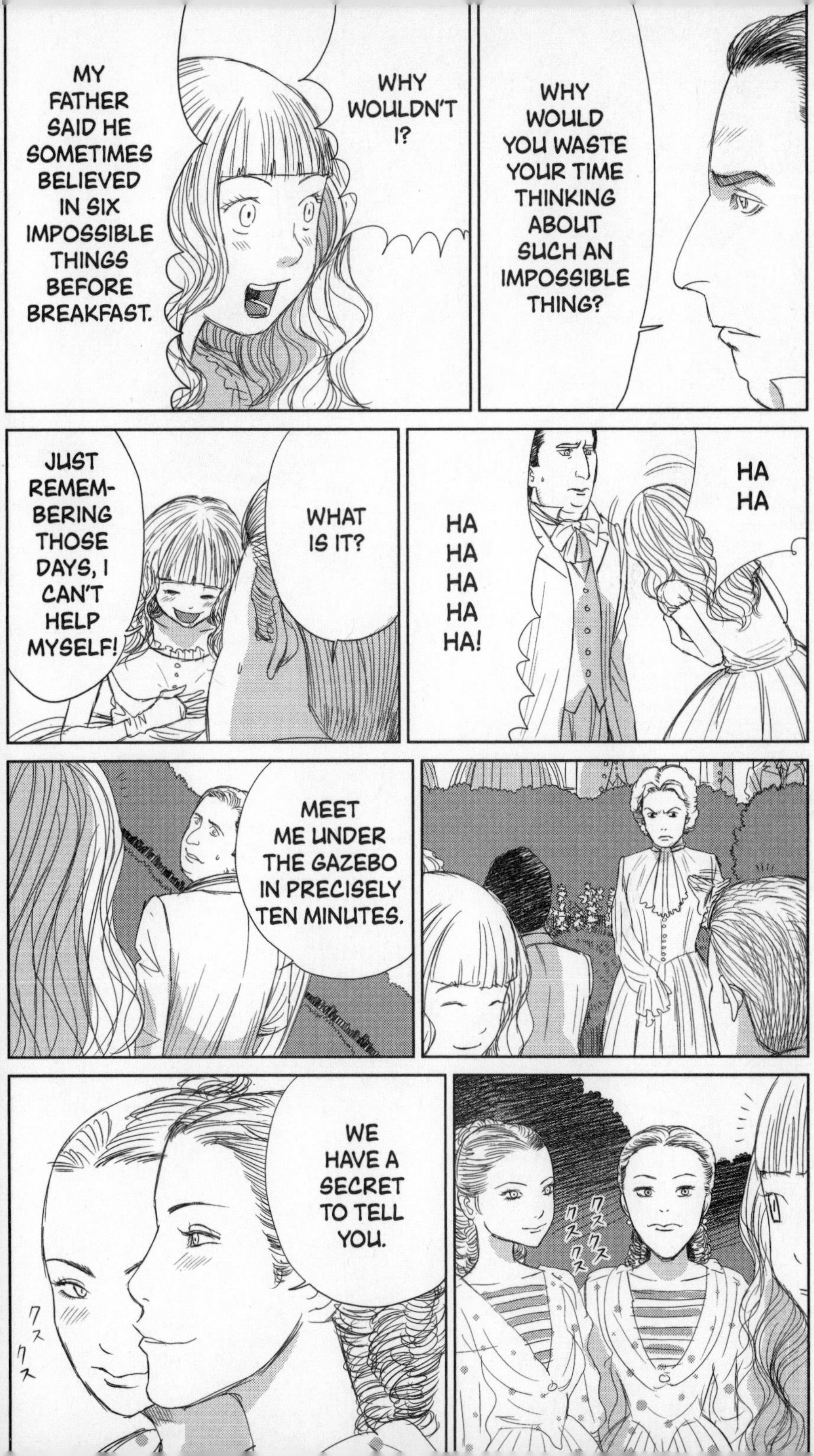
WHY WOULD YOU WASTE YOUR TIME THINKING ABOUT SUCH AN IMPOSSIBLE THING?
WHY WOULDN'T I?
MY FATHER SAID HE SOMETIMES BELIEVED IN SIX IMPOSSIBLE THINGS BEFORE BREAKFAST.
HA HA
HA HA HA HA HA!
WHAT IS IT?
JUST REMEMBERING THOSE DAYS, I CAN'T HELP MYSELF!
MEET ME UNDER THE GAZEBO IN PRECISELY TEN MINUTES.
クスクス
クスクス
WE HAVE A SECRET TO TELL YOU.
クスクス

IF WE TELL HER, SHE WON'T BE SURPRISED.
WE DECIDED WE SHOULD!
PERHAPS WE SHOULDN'T.
IF YOU'RE TELLING ME, THEN IT'S NOT MUCH OF A SECRET.
IN FACT, WE WON'T.
NO, WE DON'T.
NOT IF YOU TELL ME. BUT NOW THAT YOU'VE BROUGHT IT UP, YOU HAVE TO.
WILL YOU BE SURPRISED?
OH, BUT I WOULD. THERE'S YOUR MOTHER NOW!
YOU WOULDN'T!
I WONDER IF YOUR MOTHER KNOWS THAT YOU TWO SWIM NAKED IN THE HAVERSHIMS' POND.
DOES EVERYONE KNOW??
YOU'VE RUINED THE SURPRISE! AFTER EVERYONE WENT TO SO MUCH EFFORT TO KEEP THE SECRET...
HAMISH IS GOING TO ASK FOR YOUR HAND!

OF COURSE THEY DO.
MARGARET...
IT'S WHY THEY'VE ALL COME. THIS IS YOUR ENGAGEMENT PARTY. HAMISH WILL ASK FOR YOUR HAND UNDER THE GAZEBO.
WHEN YOU SAY "YES"...
BUT I DON'T KNOW IF I WANT TO MARRY HIM.
WHO, THEN? YOU WON'T DO BETTER THAN A LORD.
YOU'LL SOON BE TWENTY, ALICE. THAT PRETTY FACE WON'T LAST FOREVER. YOU DON'T WANT TO END UP LIKE AUNT IMOGENE.
AND YOU DON'T WANT TO BE A BURDEN ON MOTHER, DO YOU?
OF COURSE NOT...

IT'S ALREADY DECIDED.
SO YOU WILL MARRY HAMISH. YOU WILL BE AS HAPPY AS I AM WITH LOWELL AND YOUR LIFE WILL BE PERFECT.
ALICE DEAR, SHALL WE TAKE A LEISURELY STROLL THROUGH THE GARDEN?
JUST YOU AND ME?
DO YOU KNOW WHAT I'VE ALWAYS DREADED?
THE DECLINE OF THE ARISTOCRACY, LADY ASCOT?

UGLY GRANDCHILDREN. BUT YOU'RE SO LOVELY, YOU'RE BOUND TO PRODUCE LITTLE...
IMBECILES! THE GARDENERS PLANTED WHITE ROSES WHEN I SPECIFICALLY ASKED FOR RED!
YOU COULD ALWAYS PAINT THE ROSES RED.
WHAT AN ODD THING TO SAY.
COME ALONG.
チリ!
チリ!
?
YOU SHOULD KNOW THAT MY SON HAS EXTREMELY DELICATE DIGESTION...

DID YOU SEE THAT?
NASTY THINGS. I DO ENJOY SETTING THE DOGS ON THEM, THOUGH.
IT WAS A RABBIT, I THINK.
WHATEVER ARE YOU TALKING ABOUT?
IF YOU SERVE HAMISH THE WRONG FOODS, HE COULD GET A BLOCKAGE.
DON'T DAWDLE. HEAD TO THE GAZEBO.

DID YOU SEE IT THAT TIME?
SEE WHAT?
THE RABBIT!!
DON'T SHOUT! PAY ATTENTION. HAMISH SAID YOU WERE EASILY DISTRACTED.

READ THIS WAY

WHAT WAS I SAYING?
YOU WERE SAYING THAT HAMISH HAS A BLOCKAGE.
THAT'S RIGHT...
I COULDN'T BE MORE INTERESTED, BUT YOU'LL HAVE TO EXCUSE ME.
ALICE!
I'M SORRY!!
I KNOW HE CAME THIS WAY...
AAAH!
AUNT IMOGENE!!

HOW VERY STRANGE. WHAT KIND OF WAIST-COAT?
BROCADE, I THINK.
I THINK I'M GOING MAD. I KEEP SEEING A RABBIT IN A WAISTCOAT.
I CAN'T BE BOTHERED WITH YOUR FANCY RABBIT NOW. I'M WAITING FOR MY FIANCÉ.
BUT WHAT DOES IT MATTER? IT'S A RABBIT IN A WAIST-COAT!
YOU HAVE A FIANCÉ?

HE'S A PRINCE. BUT, ALAS, HE CANNOT MARRY ME UNLESS HE RENOUNCES HIS THRONE. ISN'T IT TRAGIC?
THERE! DID YOU SEE IT?
VERY.
WATCH OUT! ALICE!
WE WERE... HATTIE IS AN OLD FRIEND. YOU WON'T MENTION THIS TO YOUR SISTER, WILL YOU?

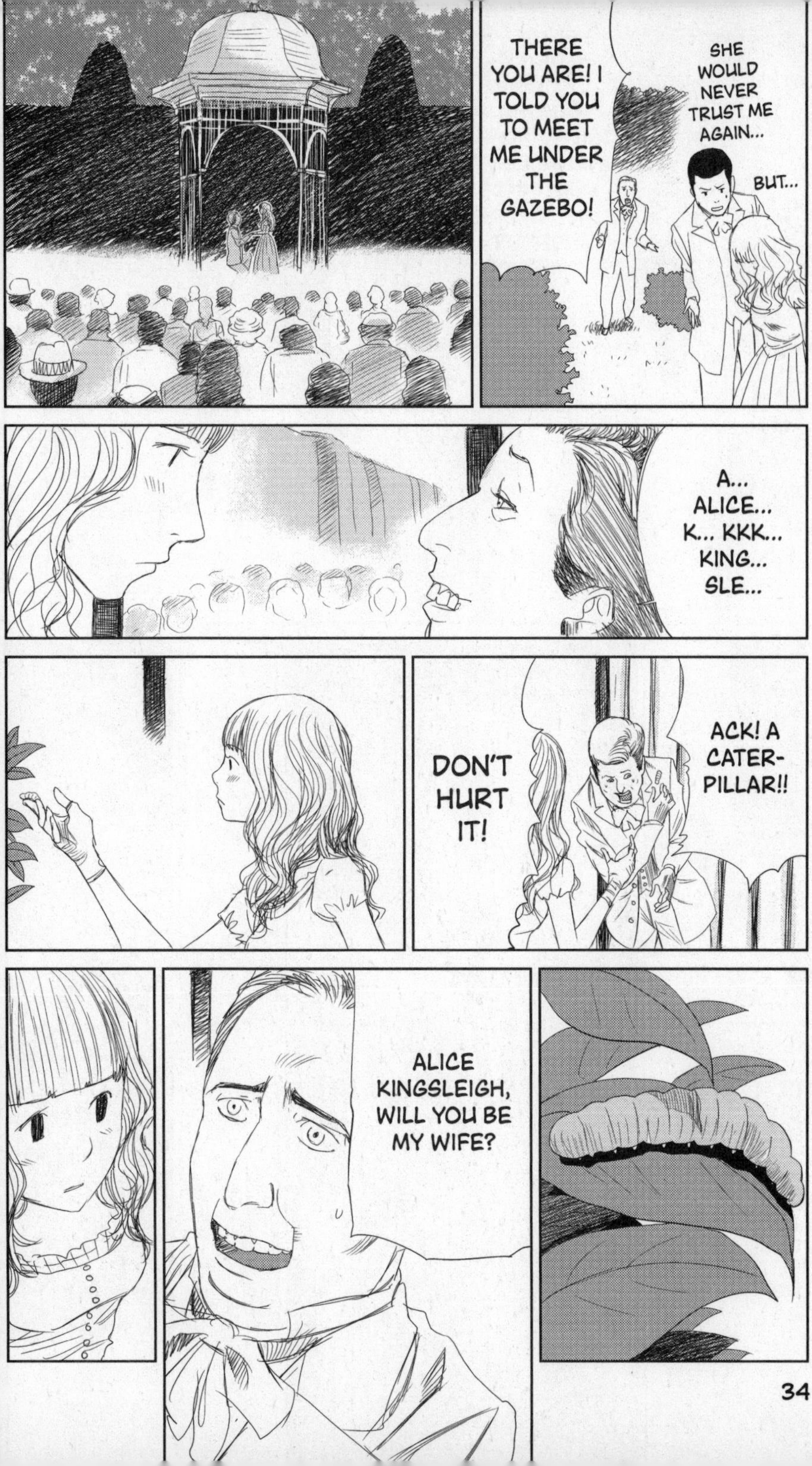
THERE YOU ARE! I TOLD YOU TO MEET ME UNDER THE GAZEBO!
SHE WOULD NEVER TRUST ME AGAIN...
BUT...
A... ALICE... K... KKK... KING... SLE...
DON'T HURT IT!
ACK! A CATER-PILLAR!!
ALICE KINGSLEIGH, WILL YOU BE MY WIFE?

I... I... WELL, EVERYONE EXPECTS ME TO...
...AND YOU'RE A LORD...
...AND MY FACE WON'T LAST...
...AND I DON'T WANT TO END UP LIKE AUNT IMOGENE...
BUT THIS IS HAPPENING SO QUICKLY.
I THINK I... I...
...I NEED A MOMENT!!
ALICE!!

ピョ
タタタ
タン
AAAAAAAH!

2 The Real Alice?

Disney

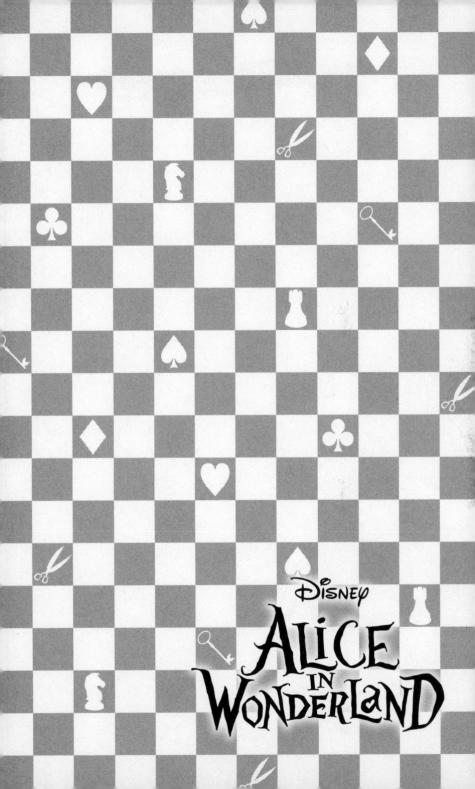

Alice in Wonderland

READ THIS WAY

ゴオオオオオオオオ

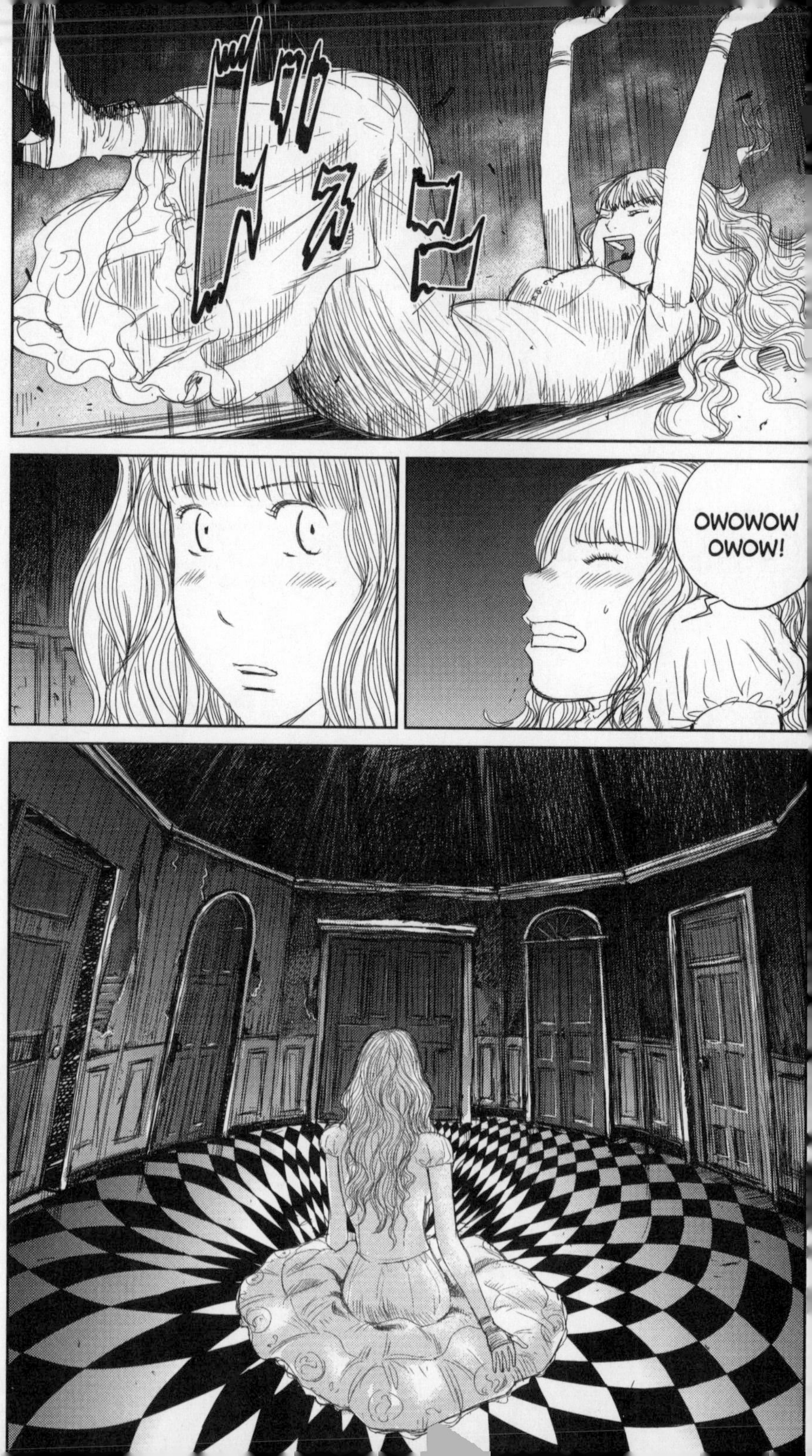
OWOWOW OWOW!

IT'S LOCKED.
THEY'RE ALL LOCKED.
THIS DOOR, TOO...
AND THIS ONE.
HELLO? IS ANYONE THERE?

?
きょろ
きょろ
スッ
カチッ
ギィーー
ゴッン
きょろ
きょろ

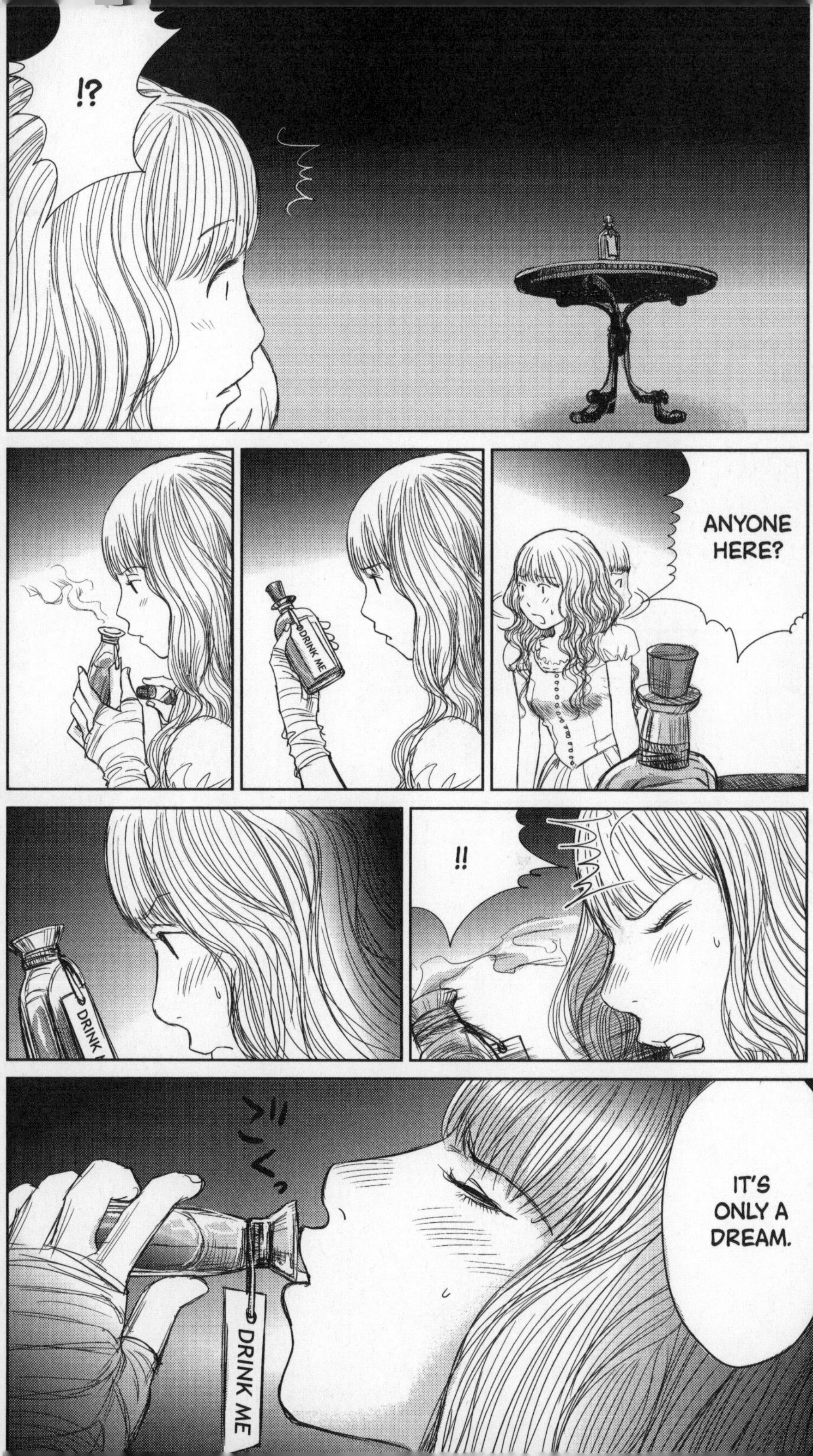
!?
ANYONE HERE?
DRINK ME
DRINK M
!!
IT'S ONLY A DREAM.
DRINK ME

バサッ
ググッ
グググググ

BEING SMALL IS FINE, BUT NOW I CAN'T REACH THE KEY.
SHE'S THE RIGHT ONE. I'M CERTAIN OF IT.
YOU'VE BROUGHT THE WRONG ALICE.
YOU'D THINK ALICE WOULD REMEMBER THIS FROM THE FIRST TIME.

ズル
ドスン
OWWW ...
?
IF THIS IS SOME SORT OF PRANK, I AM NOT AMUSED!
EAT ME

かちゃ
SHE'S THE WRONG ALICE.
GIVE HER A CHANCE...
ヒュウウウ

ガチガチガチ
ブゥウウウン
ガチガチ
SEE? I TOLD YOU SHE'S THE RIGHT ALICE.
CURIOUSER AND CURIOUSER.

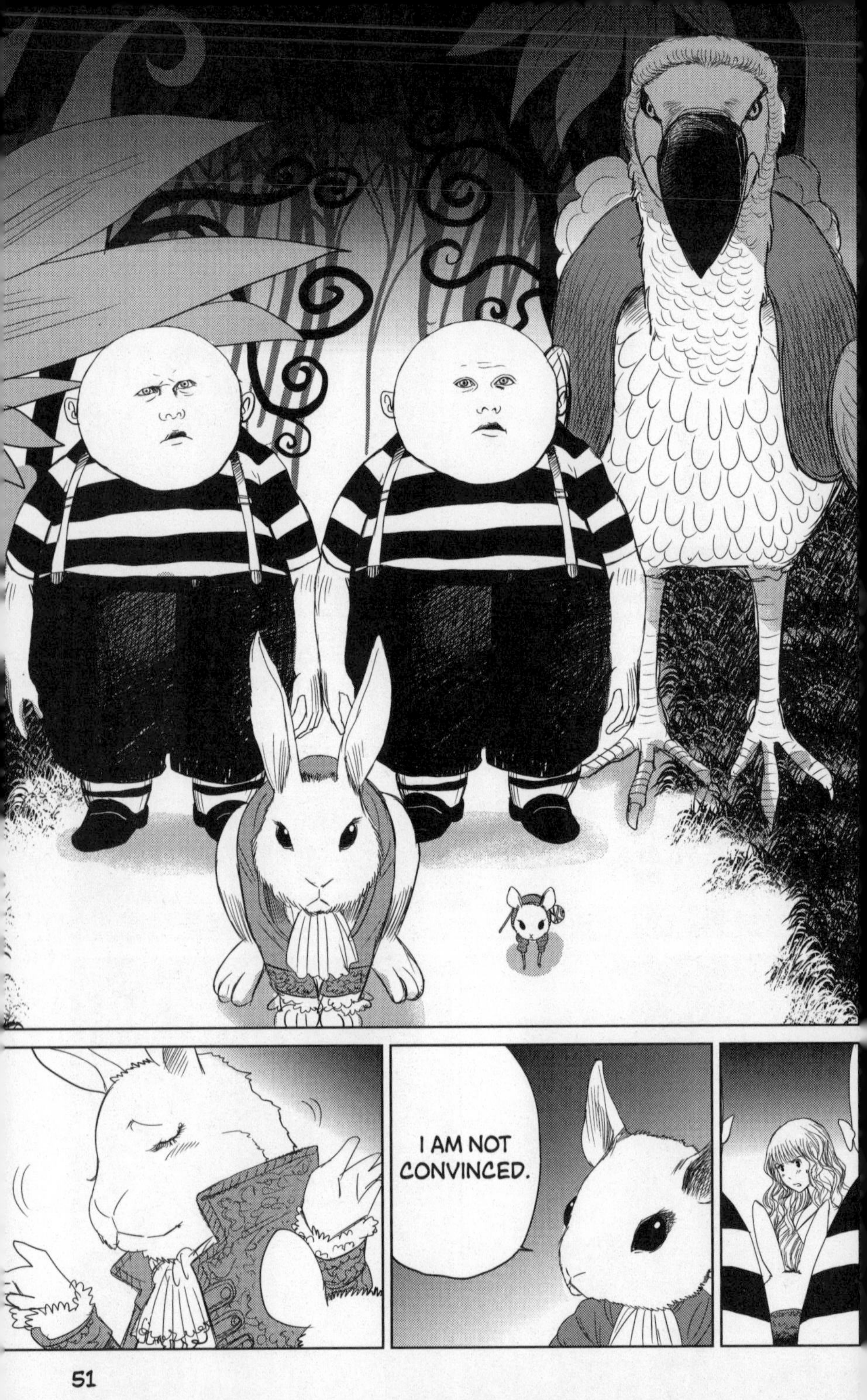
I AM NOT CONVINCED.

CAN YOU IMAGINE? THEY GO ABOUT ENTIRELY UNCLOTHED AND DO THEIR... SHUKM IN PUBLIC!
AND I WAS ALMOST EATEN BY OTHER ANIMALS!
HOW IS THAT FOR GRATITUDE? I'VE BEEN UP THERE FOR WEEKS TRAILING ONE ALICE AFTER THE NEXT!!
I HAD TO AVERT MY EYES.
SHE DOESN'T LOOK ANYTHING LIKE HERSELF.

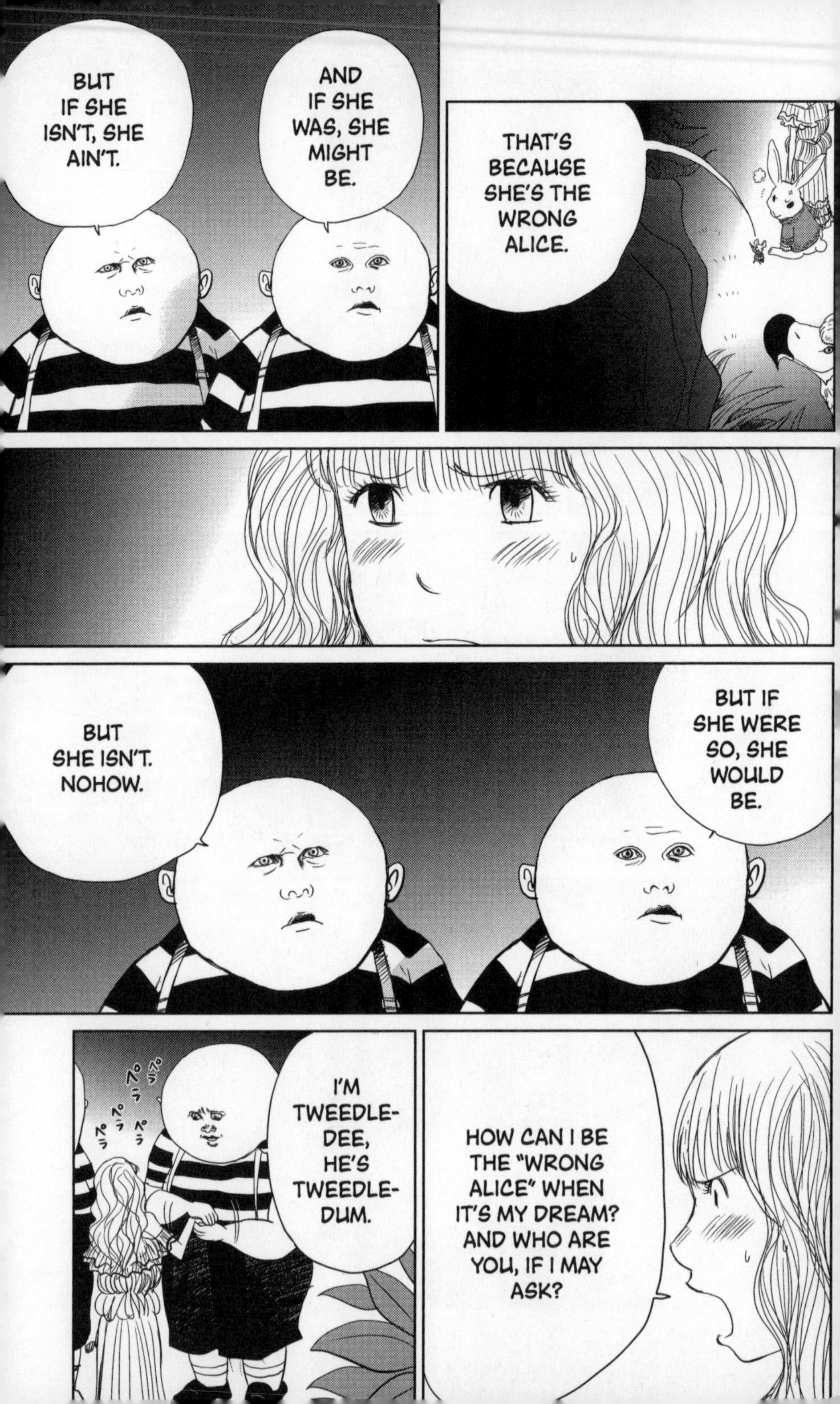
THAT'S BECAUSE SHE'S THE WRONG ALICE.
AND IF SHE WAS, SHE MIGHT BE.
BUT IF SHE ISN'T, SHE AIN'T.
BUT IF SHE WERE SO, SHE WOULD BE.
BUT SHE ISN'T. NOHOW.
HOW CAN I BE THE "WRONG ALICE" WHEN IT'S MY DREAM? AND WHO ARE YOU, IF I MAY ASK?
I'M TWEEDLE-DEE, HE'S TWEEDLE-DUM.
ペラ ペラ ペラ ペラ

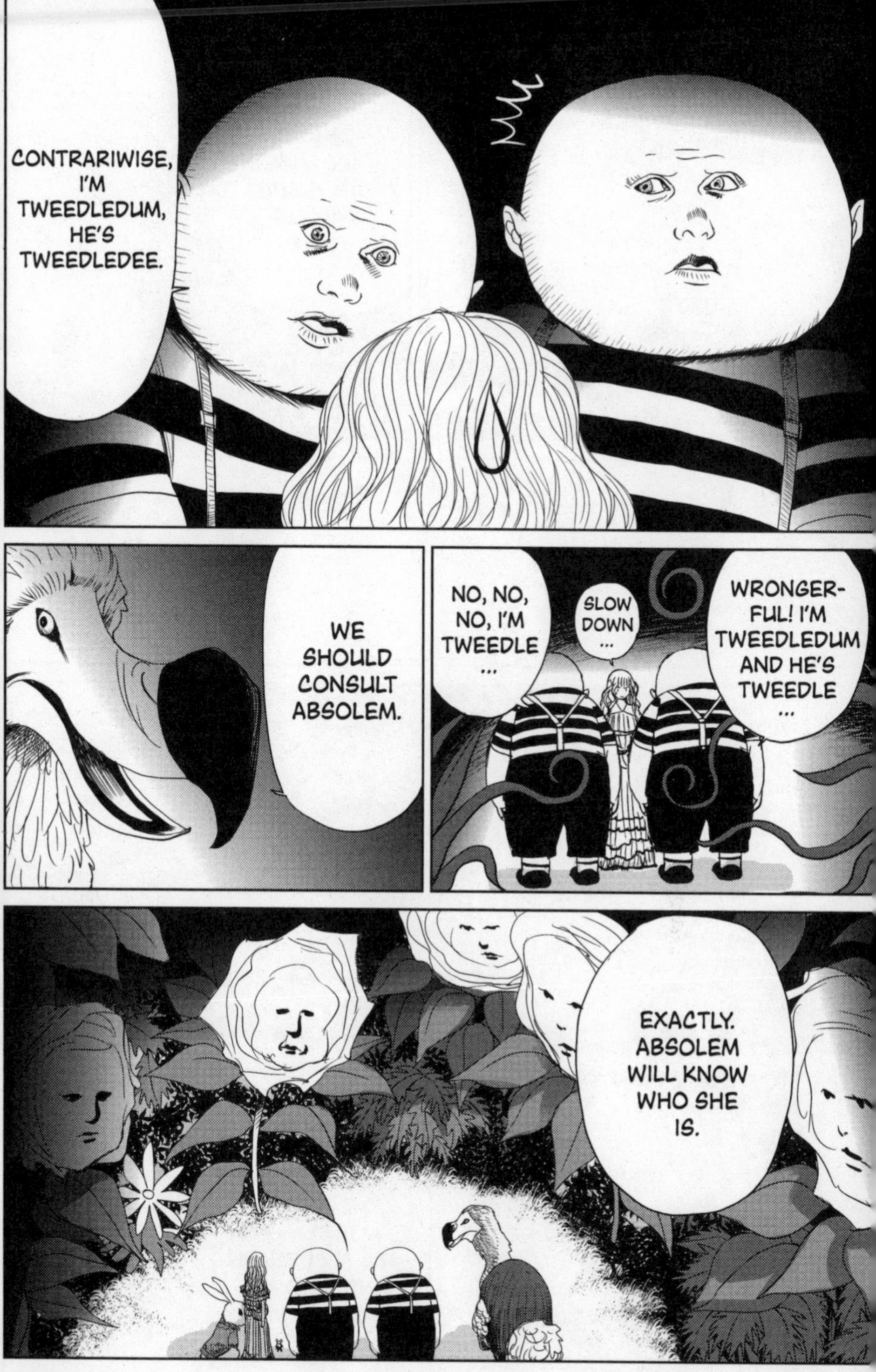
CONTRARIWISE, I'M TWEEDLEDUM, HE'S TWEEDLEDEE.
WE SHOULD CONSULT ABSOLEM.
WRONGER-FUL! I'M TWEEDLEDUM AND HE'S TWEEDLE ...
SLOW DOWN ...
NO, NO, NO, I'M TWEEDLE ...
EXACTLY. ABSOLEM WILL KNOW WHO SHE IS.

I'LL ESCORT YOU.
NO, ME...
IT'S NOT BEING YOUR TURN!!!
IT'S NOT YOUR TURN EITHER!
LEAVE OFF!
LET GO!
ARE THEY ALWAYS THIS WAY?
FAMILY TRAIT.

SHE LOOKS NOTHING LIKE ALICE.
SHE IS NOT EVEN WEARING THE RIGHT DRESS.

HE'S WISE. HE'S ABSOLUTE.
WHO IS THIS ABSOLEM?
HE'S ABSOLEM.

WHO ARE YOU?

AB...
ABSOLEM?
UH...
UH...
THE
QUESTION
IS...WHO
ARE YOU?
FOR I AM
ABSOLEM.
YOU'RE
CERTAINLY
NOT.
?

READ THIS WAY

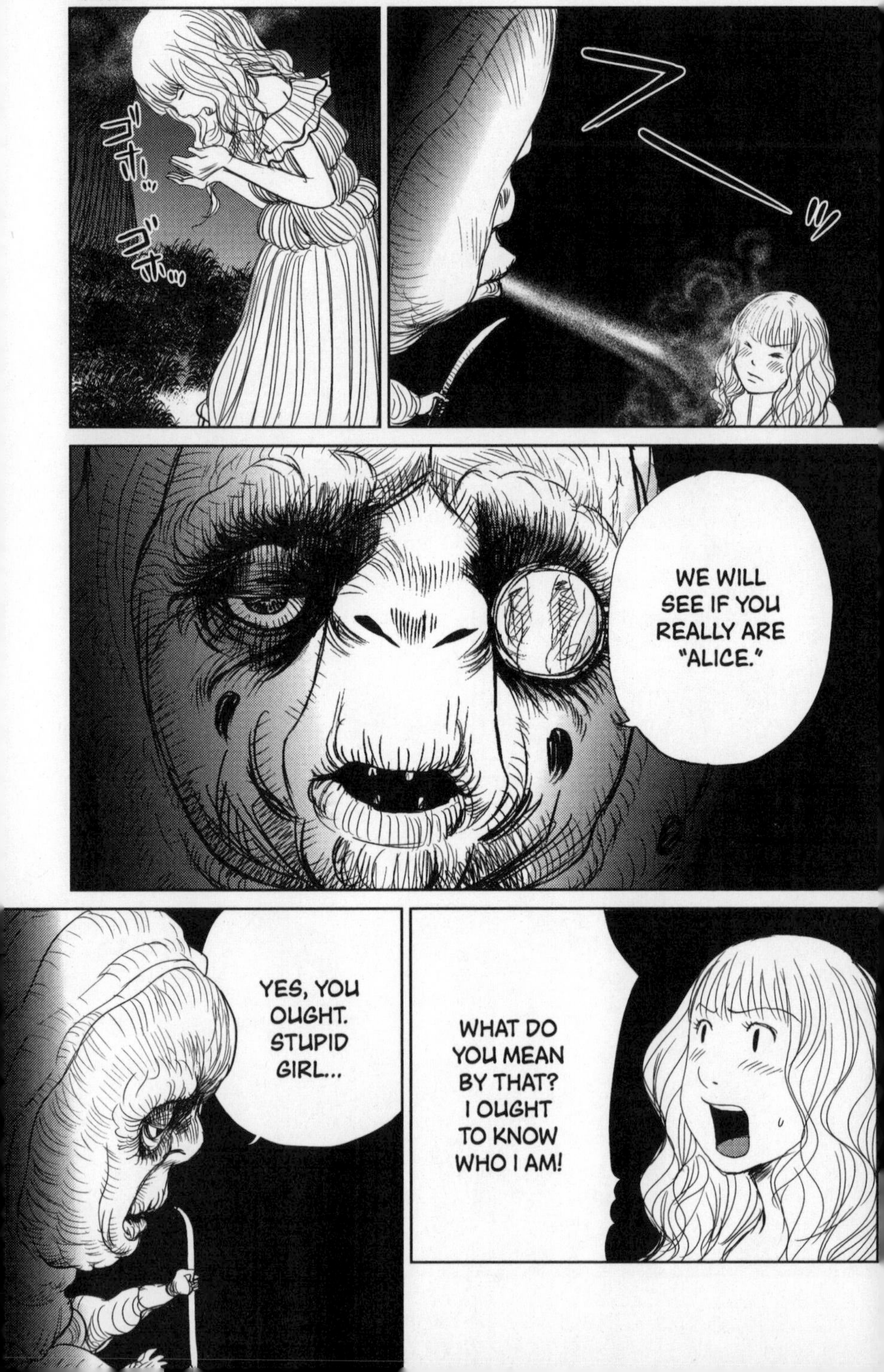

WE WILL SEE IF YOU REALLY ARE "ALICE."
WHAT DO YOU MEAN BY THAT? I OUGHT TO KNOW WHO I AM!
YES, YOU OUGHT. STUPID GIRL...

UNROLL THE ORACULUM!!
ピョン

READ THIS WAY

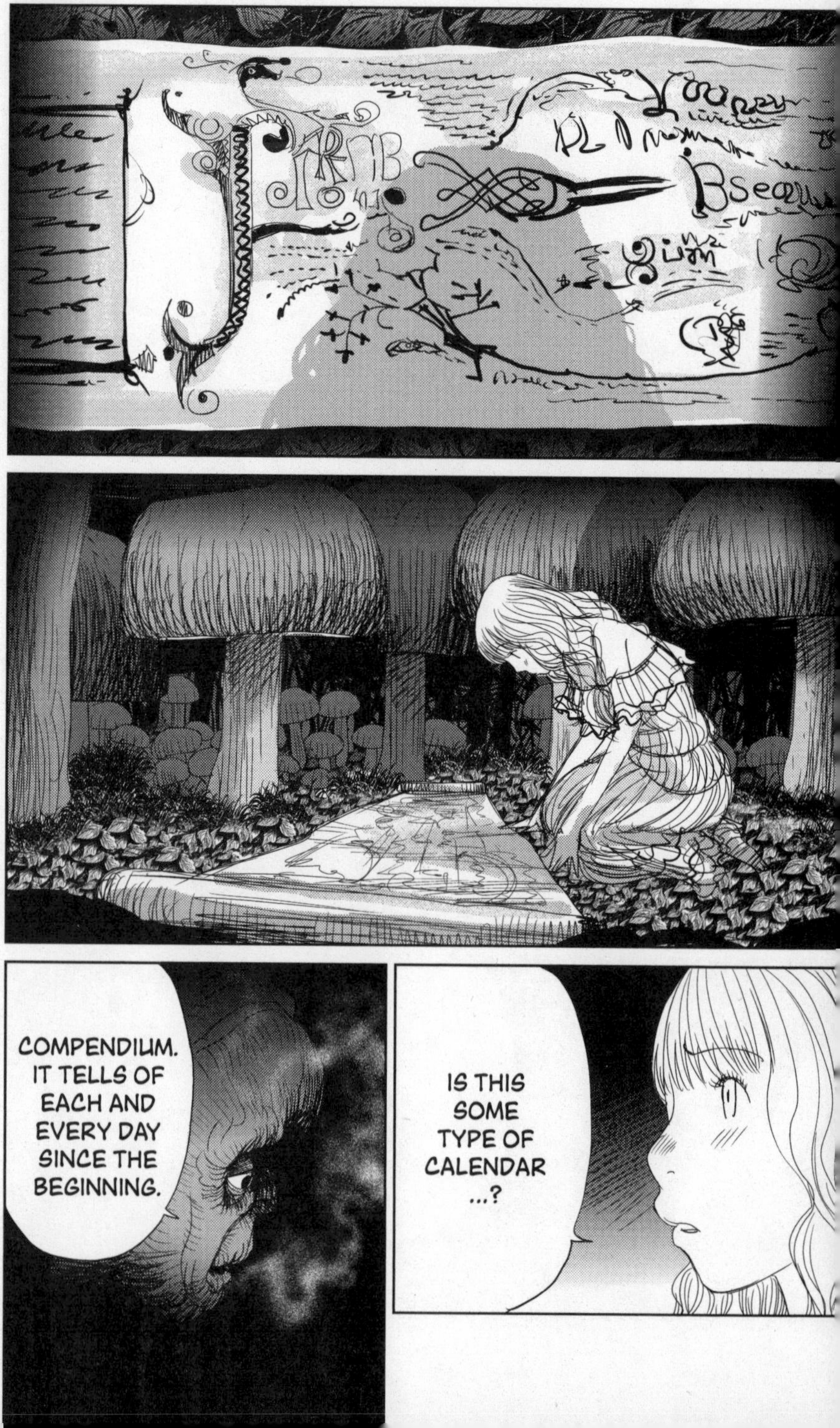
IS THIS SOME TYPE OF CALENDAR ...?
COMPENDIUM. IT TELLS OF EACH AND EVERY DAY SINCE THE BEGINNING.

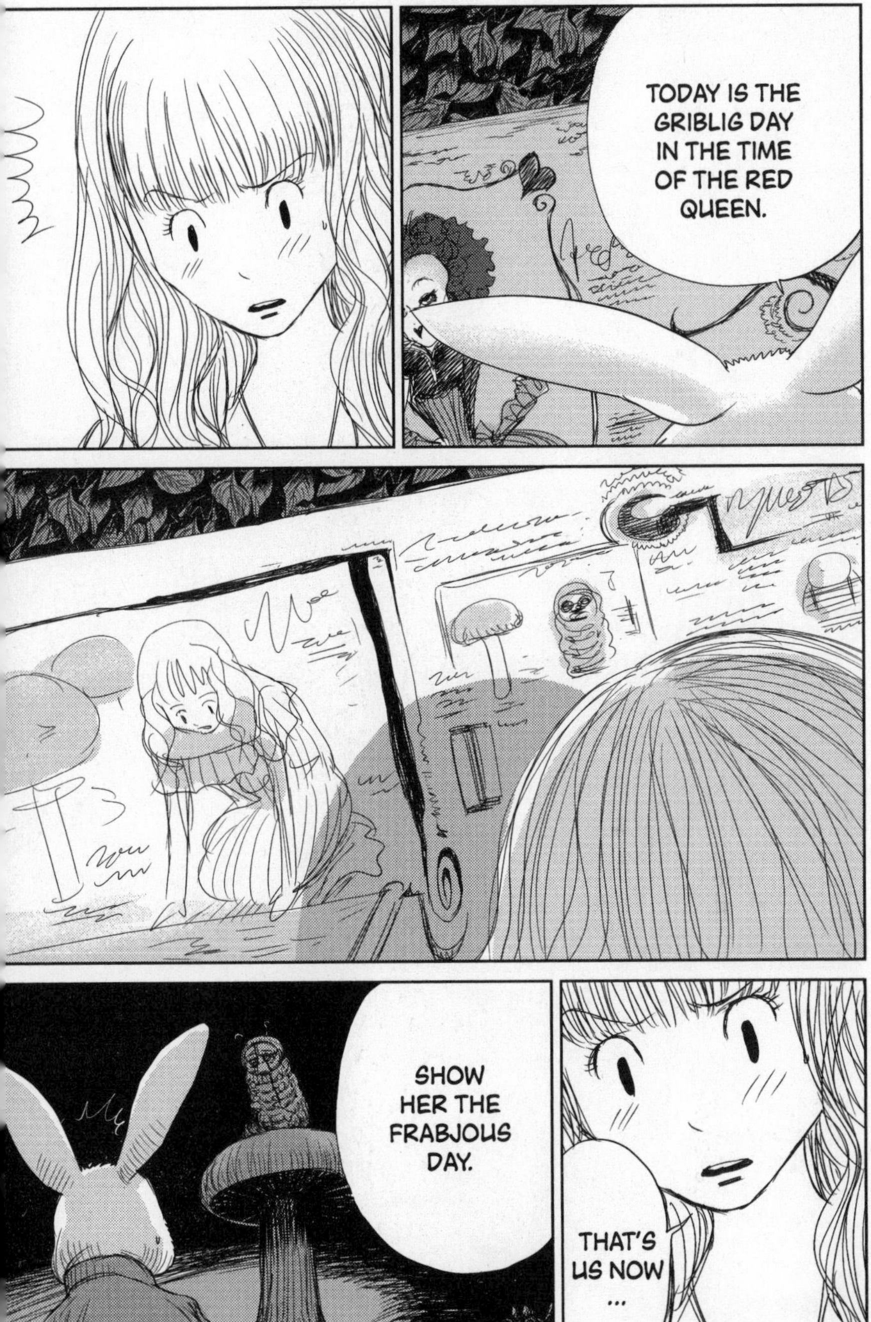
TODAY IS THE GRIBLIG DAY IN THE TIME OF THE RED QUEEN.
SHOW HER THE FRABJOUS DAY.
THAT'S US NOW ...

READ THIS WAY
ゴロッ
バサッ
THE FRABJOUS DAY IS...
THE FRABJOUS DAY IS...

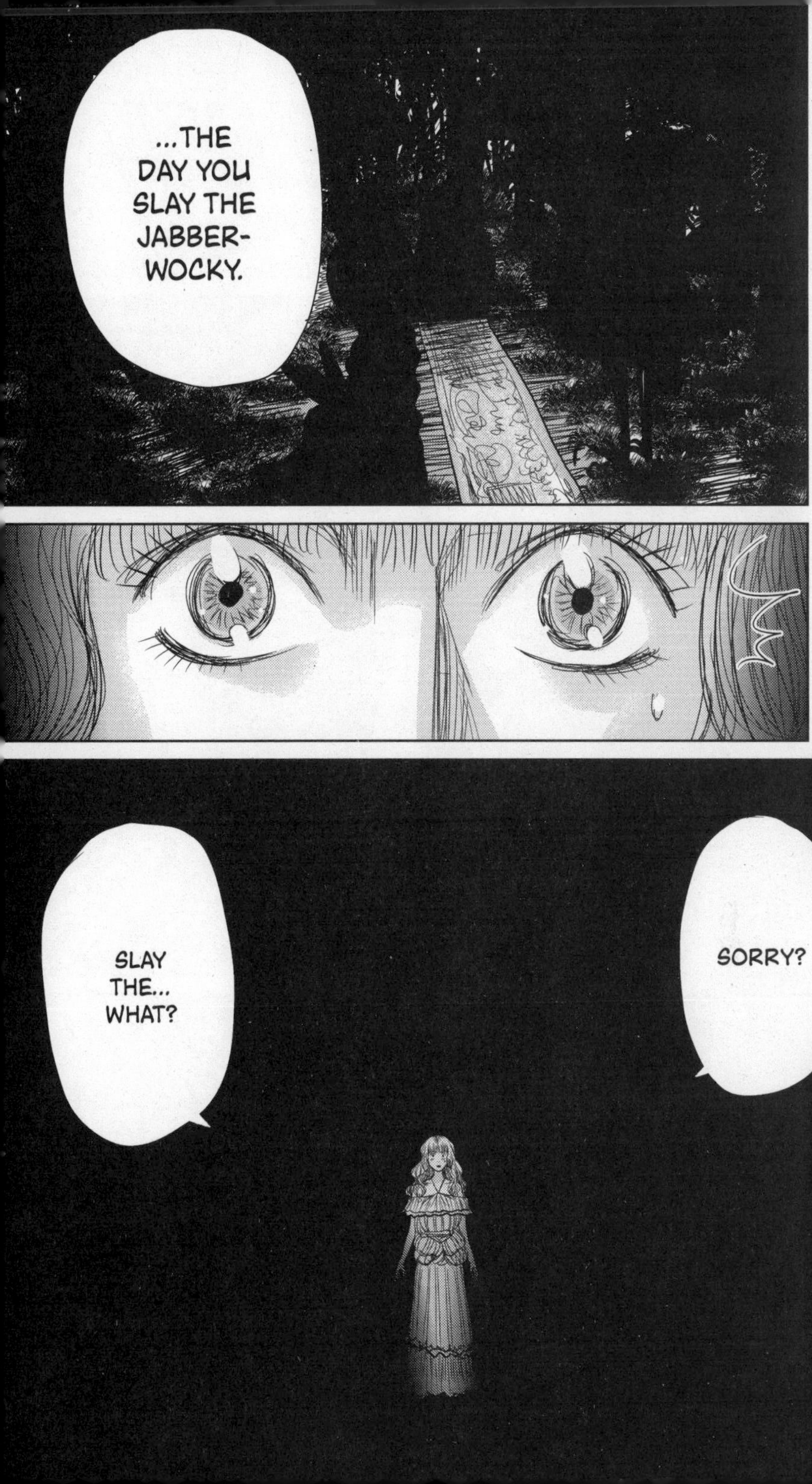
...THE DAY YOU SLAY THE JABBER-WOCKY.
SORRY?
SLAY THE... WHAT?

3 The Blind Leading the Blind

Disney

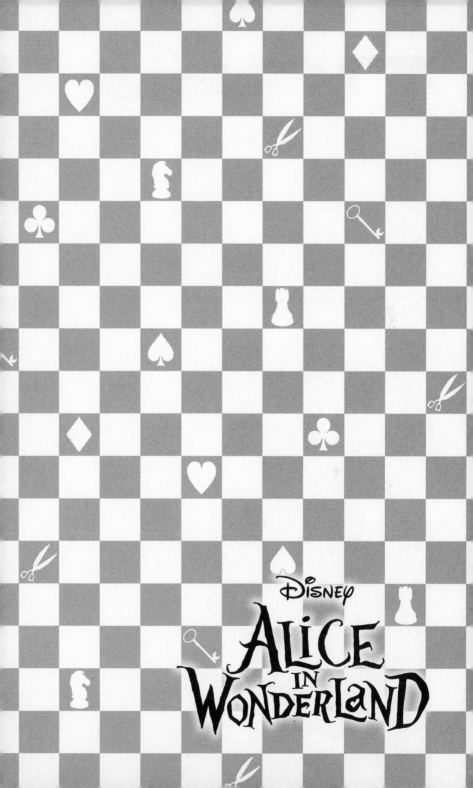

Alice in Wonderland

READ THIS WAY

カン
カン
カン

カン
カン
カン

READ THIS WAY

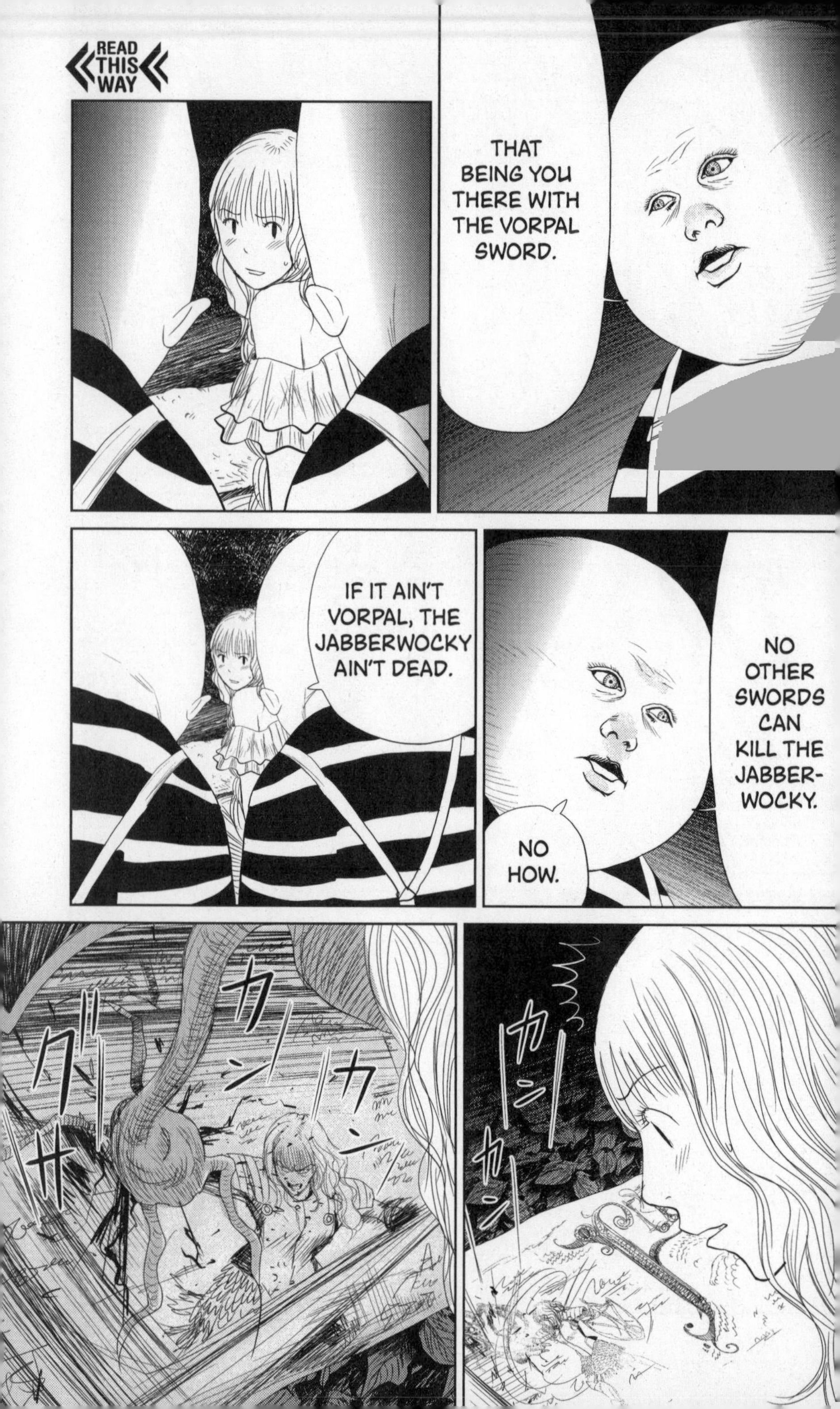

THAT BEING YOU THERE WITH THE VORPAL SWORD.
NO OTHER SWORDS CAN KILL THE JABBER-WOCKY.
NO HOW.
IF IT AIN'T VORPAL, THE JABBERWOCKY AIN'T DEAD.

!?
THAT'S NOT ME.
I KNOW!

RESOLVE THIS FOR US, ABSOLEM. IS SHE THE RIGHT ALICE?
NOT HARDLY.

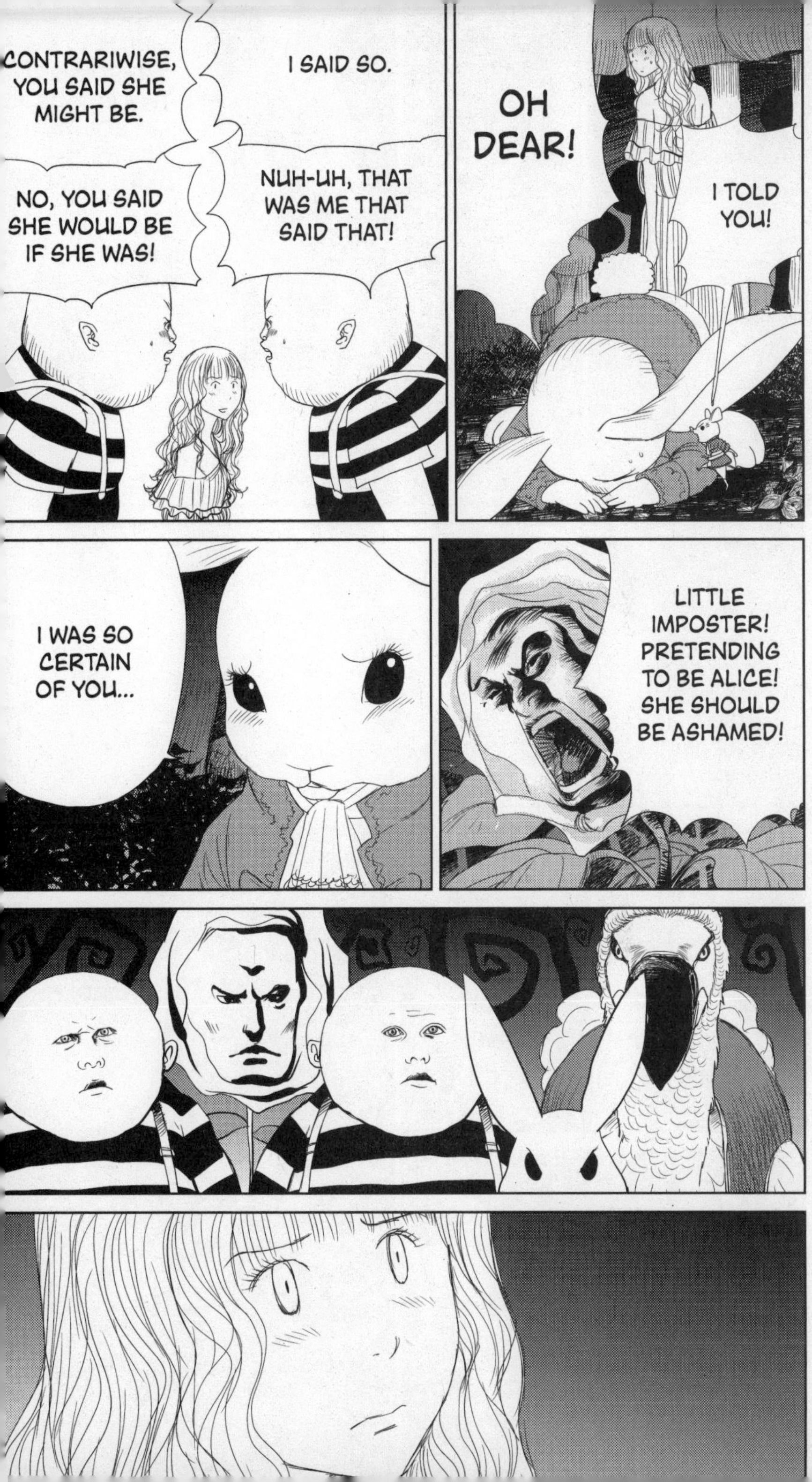
CONTRARIWISE, YOU SAID SHE MIGHT BE.
I SAID SO.
NO, YOU SAID SHE WOULD BE IF SHE WAS!
NUH-UH, THAT WAS ME THAT SAID THAT!
OH DEAR!
I TOLD YOU!
I WAS SO CERTAIN OF YOU...
LITTLE IMPOSTER! PRETENDING TO BE ALICE! SHE SHOULD BE ASHAMED!

I...I'M SORRY. I DIDN'T MEAN TO BE THE WRONG ALICE.
WAIT...
THIS IS MY DREAM. I'M GOING TO WAKE UP NOW AND YOU'LL ALL DISAPPEAR.
THAT'S CURIOUS.
PINCHING USUALLY DOES THE TRICK...

I COULD STICK YOU IF THAT WOULD HELP.
IT MIGHT ACTUALLY.
THANK YOU.
MY PLEASURE.
HAYYAA!
AAAAAAAH!
OW!
OW OW!

ゴミャアアアアアア
ガルルルルルルル
!?
ガルルルル
ジロッ
ゴミャッ
メキメキメキ

BANDER-
SNATCH!
RUN!

ガシャーン
バタバタバタバタ
UNHAND ME! I DO NOT ENJOY BEING...
パカパカ
タタンタタン

ハァ ハァ
ピタッ
WAIT, IT'S ONLY A DREAM.
NOTHING CAN HURT ME!
キッ
WHAT IS SHE DOING?

ドスッ
ブウウゥゥウ
ヌチャ
ヌチャ
ガオオオオ
CAN'T HURT ME...
CAN'T HURT ME...

YOU GREAT LUG!
HURRY UP AND RUN!
ヒョッ
シュッ
グッ

!!
RUN, I SAY!

HYAH!

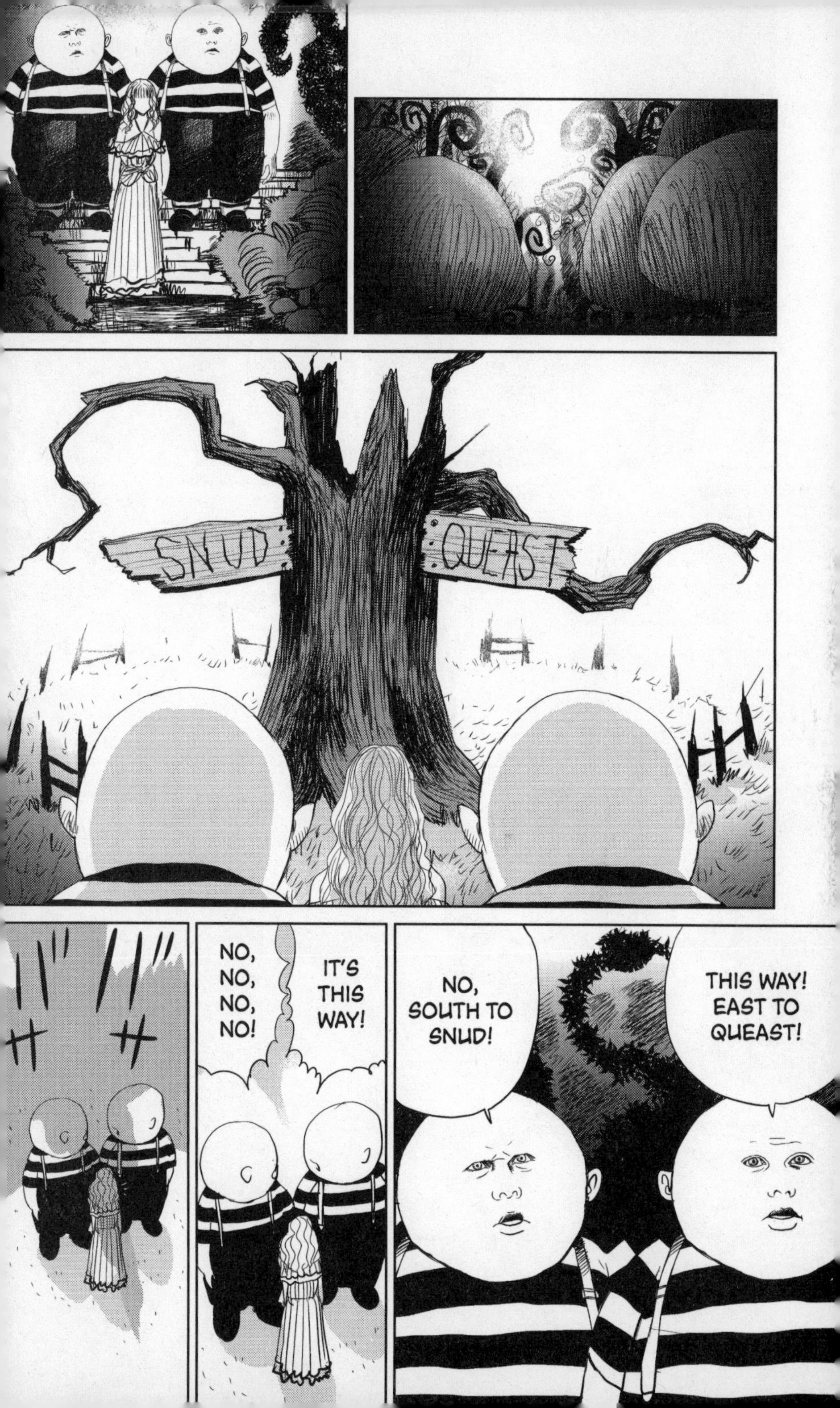
SNUD
QUEAST
NO, NO, NO, NO!
IT'S THIS WAY!
NO, SOUTH TO SNUD!
THIS WAY! EAST TO QUEAST!

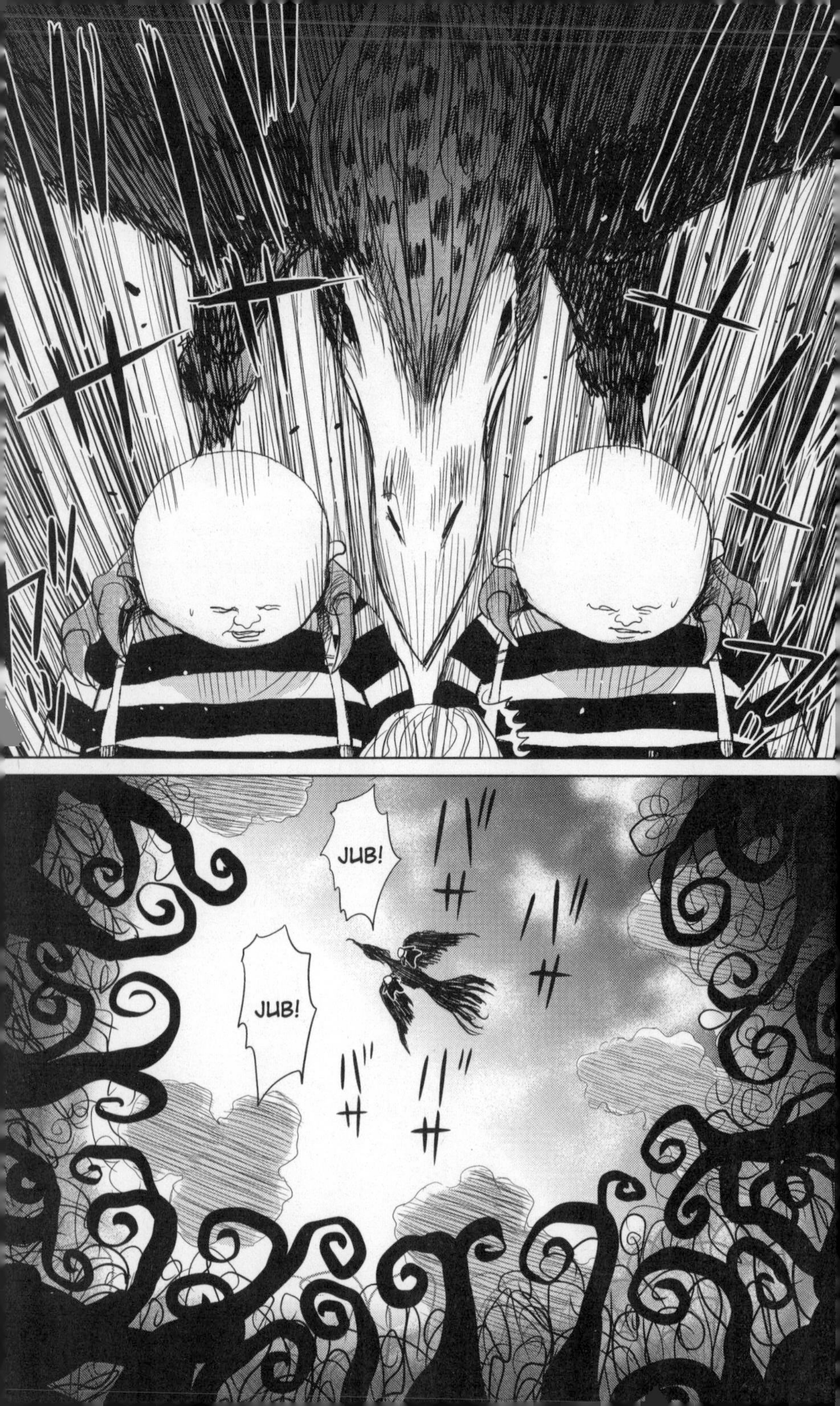
JUB!
JUB!

SOMEONE STOLE THREE OF MY TARTS!
DID YOU STEAL THEM?!
NO, YOUR MAJESTY!

READ THIS WAY
キッ
DID YOU STEAL MY TARTS?
N...NO, YOUR MA...M... MAJESTY.
SQUIMBERRY JUICE.
カッ
I WAS SO HUNGRY!
OFF WITH HIS HEAD!

NO! PLEASE! I HAVE LITTLE ONES TO LOOK AFTER!
GO TO HIS HOUSE AND COLLECT THE LITTLE ONES!
I LOVE TADPOLES ON TOAST POINTS ALMOST AS MUCH AS I LOVE CAVIAR.
AA AA HA HA HA HA HA!
MAJESTY?
ILOSOVIC STAYNE... YOU KNAVE! WHERE HAVE YOU BEEN LURKING? ♡
す
チュッ

MAJESTY, I FOUND THE ORACULUM.
THAT? IT LOOKS SO ORDINARY FOR AN ORACLE.
LOOK HERE, ON THE FRABJOUS DAY.
I'D KNOW THAT TANGLED MESS OF HAIR ANY-WHERE.
IS IT ALICE?
I BELIEVE IT IS.
WHAT IS SHE DOING WITH MY DARLING JABBERWOCKY?
SHE APPEARS TO BE SLAYING IT.
ALICE KILLED MY JABBER-BABY-WOCKY?
NOT YET.
BUT IT WILL HAPPEN IF WE DON'T STOP HER.
!?

FIND ALICE, STAYNE. FIND HER!
I WILL BRING HER HEAD AND LAY IT AT YOUR FEET.
NO. BRING THE WHOLE GIRL.
I WANT TO DO IT MYSELF!
FIND THE SCENT OF THAT HUMAN GIRL AND EARN YOUR FREEDOM.

FOR MY WIFE AND PUPS AS WELL?
EVERYONE GOES HOME.
スタッ
くんくん
DOGS WILL BELIEVE ANYTHING.
くんくん
ハァ ハァ
IT LOOKS LIKE YOU RAN AFOUL OF SOMETHING WITH WICKED CLAWS.
?

ぬっ

AAAAH!
?
AND I'M STILL DREAMING!
WHAT DID THAT TO YOU?
THE BANNER... OR BANDER...
ニョロ〜
THE BAND-ERSNATCH? I'D BETTER HAVE A LOOK.
スッ
!!

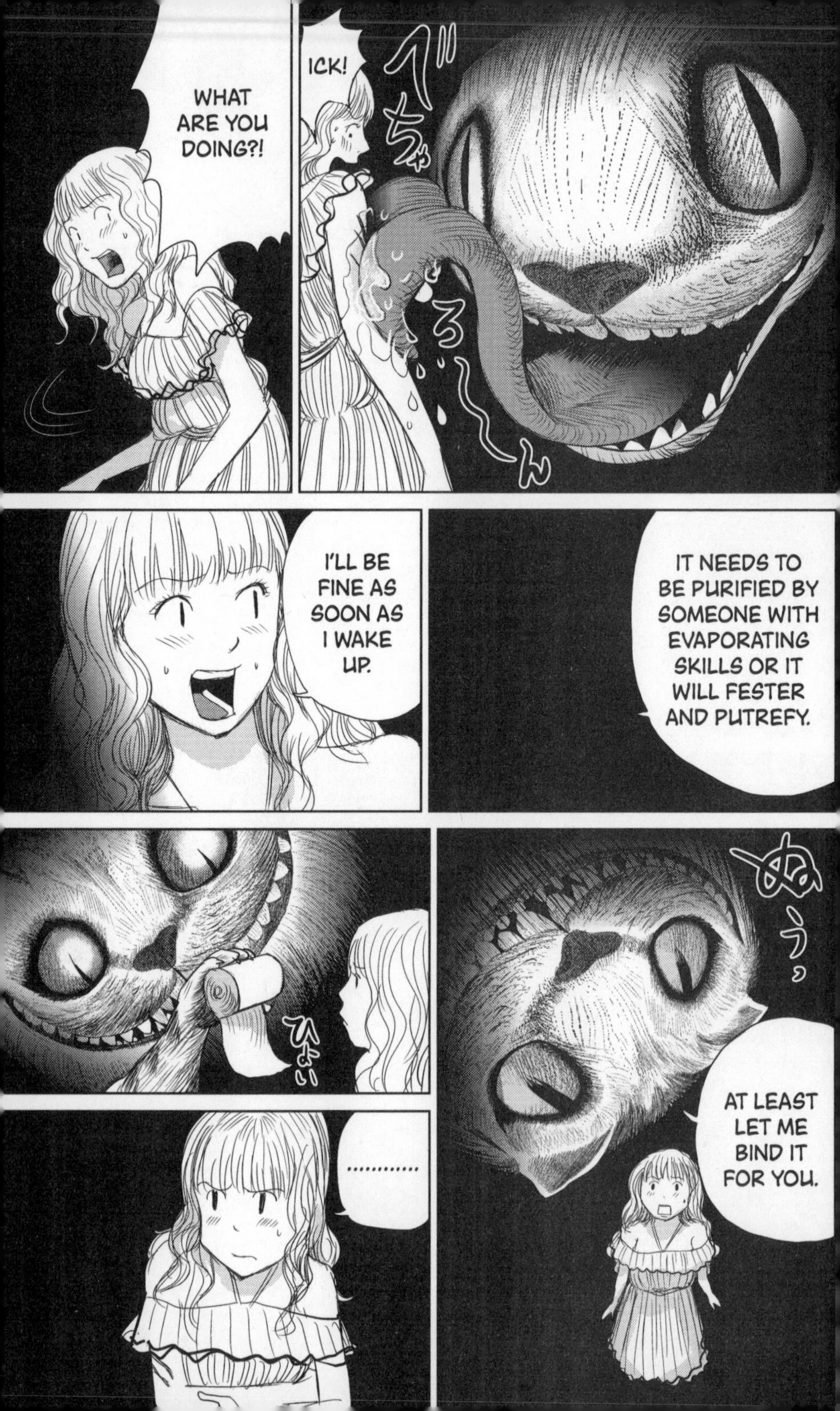

べちゃ
ICK!
WHAT ARE YOU DOING?!
IT NEEDS TO BE PURIFIED BY SOMEONE WITH EVAPORATING SKILLS OR IT WILL FESTER AND PUTREFY.
I'LL BE FINE AS SOON AS I WAKE UP.
ぬぅっ
AT LEAST LET ME BIND IT FOR YOU.
ひょい
....

ぐる
ぐる
WHAT DO YOU CALL YOURSELF?
ALICE.
THE ALICE?
!?

I'M NOT GOING INTO THAT AGAIN!
I NEVER GET INVOLVED IN POLITICS. YOU'D BEST BE ON YOUR WAY.
WHAT WAY? ALL I WANT TO DO IS WAKE UP FROM THIS DREAM!
FINE. I'LL TAKE YOU TO THE HARE AND THE HATTER.

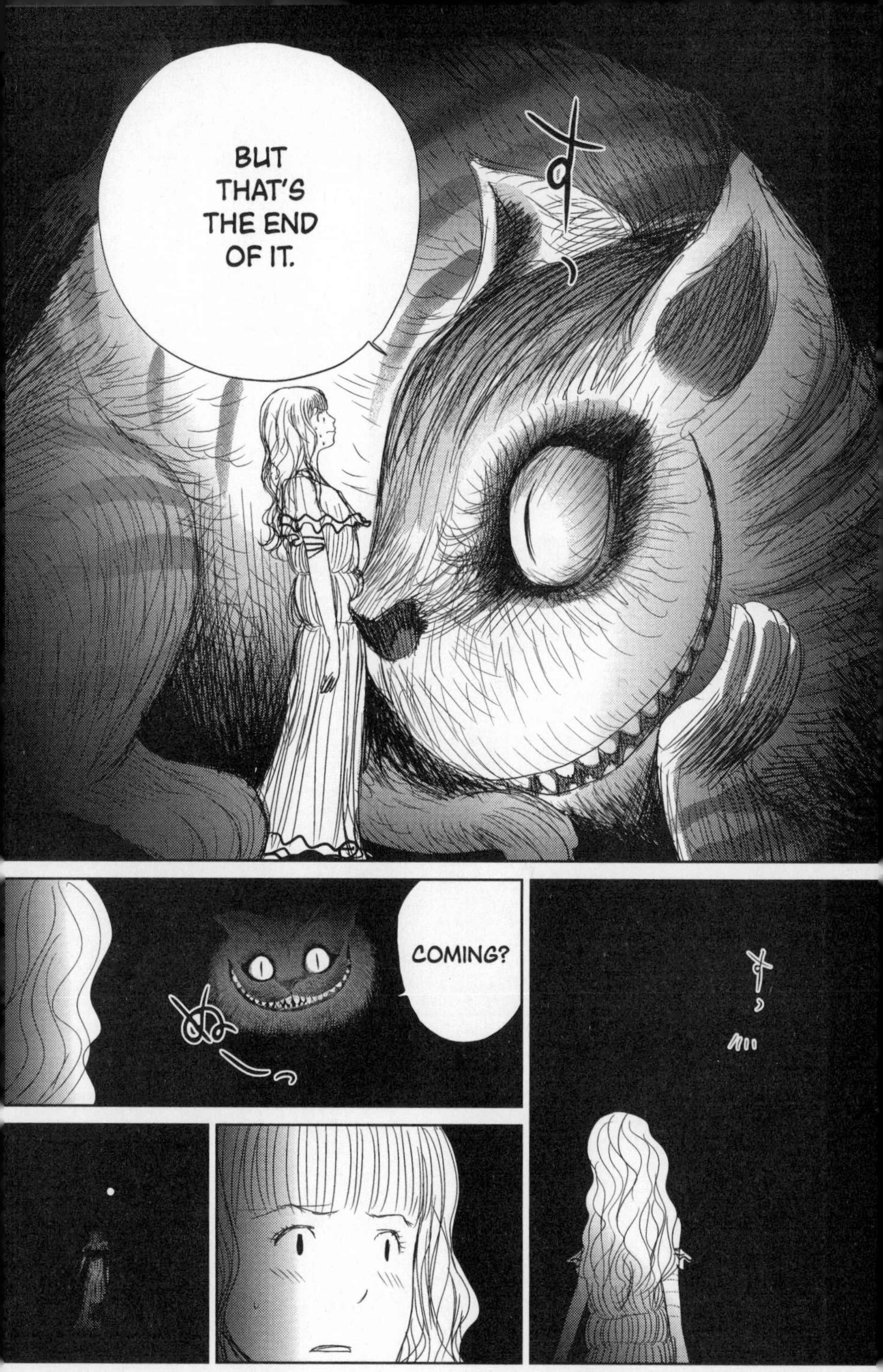
BUT THAT'S THE END OF IT.
COMING?

4 Mad Hatter Appears

Disney

Alice in Wonderland

READ THIS WAY

ボーッ

READ THIS WAY

グクン
つん
つん
WHAT? WHERE?
WHO'S THERE?
ボワン
スッ

シャキン
ガシャン
ガッ
ガシャン
ガシャン
ガッ
ガシャン

IT'S ALICE!
NO, IT'S NOT. MCTWISP BROUGHT US THE WRONG ALICE.
IT'S ABSOLUTELY ALICE!
I'D KNOW YOU ANYWHERE! I'D KNOW HER ANYWHERE, YOU KNOW.

HEY!
!?
すっ

WELL, AS YOU CAN SEE, WE'RE STILL HAVING TEA.
IT'S ALL BECAUSE I WAS OBLIGED TO KILL TIME WAITING FOR YOUR RETURN.
TIME BECAME QUITE OFFENDED AND STOPPED ALTOGETHER.
TIME CAN BE FUNNY IN DREAMS.
BUT NOW THAT YOU'RE BACK, WE NEED TO GET ON TO THE FRABJOUS DAY!
DOWNAL WYTH BLUDDY BEHG HID!

BLOODY BIG HEAD BEING THE RED QUEEN.
"DOWN WITH THE BLOODY BIG HEAD."
SORRY?
COME, COME. WE SIMPLY MUST COMMENCE WITH THE SLAYING AND SUCH...
IT'S SOMETHING OF A SLOGAN FOR THE UNDERLAND UNDERGROUND RESISTANCE!
IT'S A SECRET LANGUAGE USED BY US.
とん
とん
コチ
カチ
カチ
ジャブ
ジャブ
IT'S HIGH TIME FOR TIME TO FORGIVE AND FORGET!

ALL THIS TALK OF BLOOD AND SLAYING HAS PUT ME OFF MY TEA.
IT'S TICKING AGAIN!!
WHAT HAPPENED THAT DAY WAS NOT MY FAULT!
THE ENTIRE WORLD IS FALLING TO RUIN AND POOR CHESSUR'S OFF HIS TEA...
YOU RAN OUT ON THEM TO SAVE YOUR OWN SKIN!

YOU GUDDLER'S SCUTTISH PILGAR LICKERING ...
... SLURKINGUR-PALSLACKUSH SCRUMSNOKING PEWGULLGAMMER MUCKFLOTCH-FIGERIFIC...
HATTER!

READ THIS WAY
THANK YOU. I'M FINE.
WHAT'S WRONG WITH YOU, TARRANT? YOU USED TO BE THE LIFE OF THE PARTY. YOU USED TO BE THE BEST FUTTERWACKEN IN ALL OF WITZEND.
FUTTER...?
IT'S A DANCE.
ON THE FRABJOUS DAY, WHEN THE WHITE QUEEN WEARS THE CROWN AGAIN. ON THAT DAY, I'LL FUTTERWACKEN...

HMM?
つん
つん
IT'S THE KNAVE!
HIDE HER!
DRINK THIS.
OH NO...
HURRY UP AND DRINK!
ゴクッ
ポイッ
かちゃ

YOU'RE ALL LATE FOR TEA!
WELL, IF IT'S NOT MY FAVORITE TRIO OF LUNATICS.
ぱか ぱか
ぱか ぱか
WE'RE LOOKING FOR THE GIRL CALLED ALICE.

SPEAKING OF THE QUEEN, HERE'S A SONG WE SANG AT HER SOIRÉE.
ONE, TWO, THREE ♪
TWINKLE, TWINKLE ♪
LITTLE BAT! ♫

HOW I WONDER ♪
WHERE YOU'RE AT ♫
IF YOU'RE HIDING HER, YOU'LL LOSE YOUR HEADS.
ALREADY LOST THEM. ALL SING TOGETHER!
UP ABOVE THE WORLD YOU FLY, LIKE A TEA TRAY IN THE SKY
A A A A A

くんくん
くんくん
TWINKLE
TWINKLE
TWINKLE
TWINKLE
♪

DOWNAL WYTH BLUDDY BEHG HID
スタッ
タタッ
FOLLOW THE BLOODHOUND!
YOU'RE ALL MAD...

HATTER!!
I'M FINE.
REALLY,
I'M FINE.

AAAAH!
ぱか
SORRY...
カチャ
ONE MOMENT!
チョキチョキ
ぬいぬいぬいぬい

かちゃ
KNOCK, KNOCK!
TRY THIS ON FOR SIZE.
チャッ
SORRY, IT'S THE BEST I COULD DO!
BUUUT... NOT AS GOOD AS I HAD BEEN HOPING EITHER.
NOT HALF BAD, NOT HALF BAD AT ALL!

READ THIS WAY

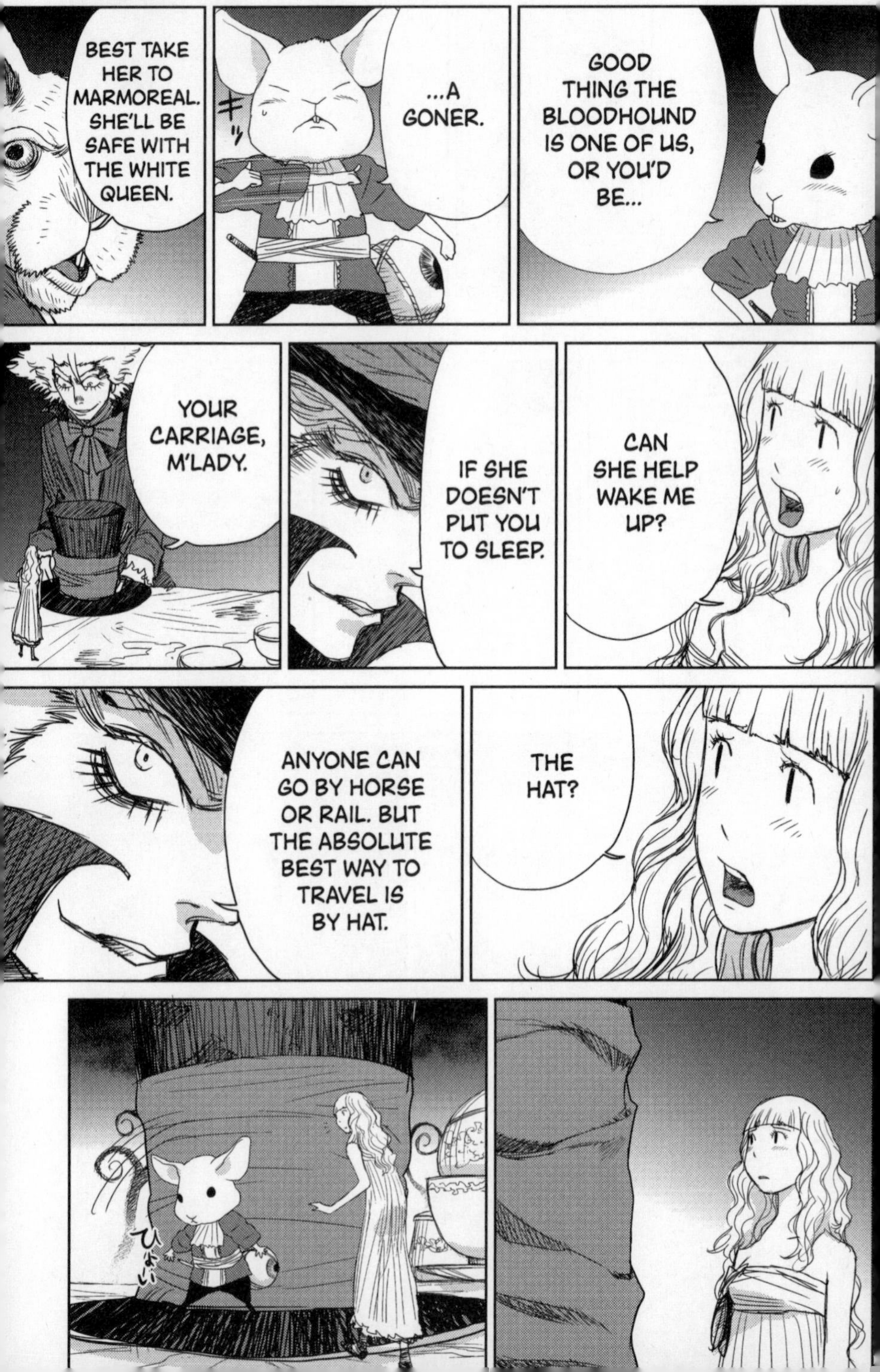
GOOD THING THE BLOODHOUND IS ONE OF US, OR YOU'D BE...
...A GONER.
キッ
BEST TAKE HER TO MARMOREAL. SHE'LL BE SAFE WITH THE WHITE QUEEN.
CAN SHE HELP WAKE ME UP?
IF SHE DOESN'T PUT YOU TO SLEEP.
YOUR CARRIAGE, M'LADY.
THE HAT?
ANYONE CAN GO BY HORSE OR RAIL. BUT THE ABSOLUTE BEST WAY TO TRAVEL IS BY HAT.
ひょい

SORRY, MALLY, JUST ALICE.
FAIR-FARREN, ALL!
BUT YOU HAVEN'T HAD YOUR TEA!
MIND YOUR HEAD.

'TWAS BRILLING AND THE SLITHY TOVES
DID GYRE AND GIMBLE IN THE WABE.
ALL MIMSY WERE THE BOROGROVES,
AND THE MOME RATHS OUTGRABE.
SORRY, WHAT WAS THAT?
IT'S A TALE FROM THE OUTLANDS. IT'S ALL ABOUT YOU, YOU KNOW.
THE VORPAL BLADE WENT SNICKER-SNACK. HE LEFT IT DEAD, AND WITH ITS HEAD. AND HE WENT GALUMPHING BACK.
I'M NOT SLAYING ANYTHING. I DON'T SLAY. SO PUT IT OUT OF YOUR MIND!
MMM... MIND.

YOU CAN'T LEAVE ME HERE!
WAIT!
YOU "DON'T SLAY."
DO YOU HAVE ANY IDEA WHAT THE RED QUEEN HAS DONE?
BUT IT HAS NOTHING TO DO WITH YOU, RIGHT?
YOU'RE NOT THE SAME AS YOU WERE BEFORE. YOU WERE MUCH MORE... MUCH MORE... MUCHIER. YOU'VE LOST YOUR MUCHNESS.
I COULDN'T IF I WANTED TO.

MY "MUCHNESS"?
IN THERE.
SOME-THING'S MISSING.
TELL ME WHAT THE RED QUEEN HAS DONE.
IT'S NOT A PRETTY STORY.
TELL ME ANYWAY.

I WAS HATTER TO THE QUEEN AT THE TIME. THE HIGHTOPP CLAN HAVE ALWAYS BEEN EMPLOYED AT COURT.

5 To the Red Queen's Castle

Disney
ALICE
IN
WONDERLAND

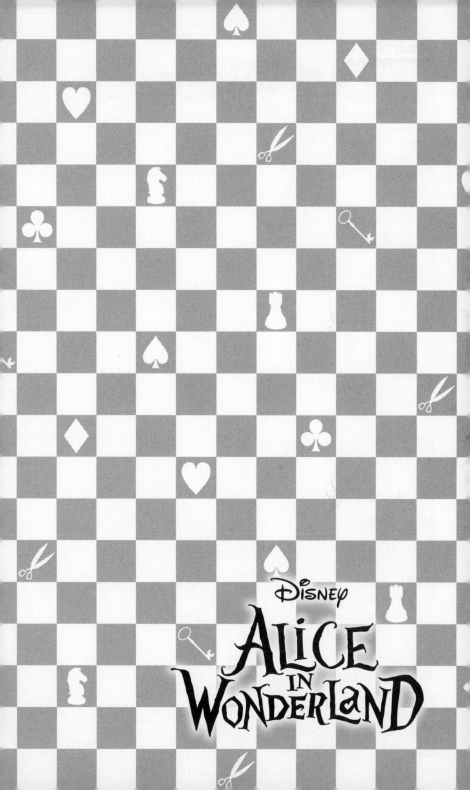

READ THIS WAY

I WAS THE WHITE QUEEN'S HATTER, YES.
THE HIGHTOPP CLAN HAVE ALWAYS BEEN EMPLOYED BY THE COURT.
WE WERE IN THE TULGEY WOOD... IT WAS THE HORUNVENDUSH DAY.
THE MOOD WAS FESTIVE AND MARCH HARE, CHESSUR CAT, AND WHITE RABBIT WERE ALL THERE MINGLING.
JUST THEN, THESE LARGE, LEATHERY WINGS SWOOPED IN AND BLOCKED OUT THE SUN.
THE WOOD WAS PLUNGED INTO DARKNESS.

A TERRIFYING BEAST, THE JABBERWOCKY, DESCENDED UPON US AND STARTED BREATHING FIRE ON EVERYTHING.

EVERY TIME THE JABBERWOCKY WOULD BREATHE ITS FIRE...
...PEOPLE WOULD SCAMPER AWAY IN A PANIC.

I ESCORTED THE WHITE QUEEN TO SAFETY...
...WHILE WHITE RABBIT HELPED EVERYONE ELSE SEEK REFUGE.
MARCH HARE WAS FROZEN FROM THE SHOCK.
ALL HE COULD DO WAS LOOK UP TO THE SKY.

READ THIS WAY

THE HIGHTOPP CLAN WERE TRYING TO PROTECT THE CHILDREN WHILE CHESSUR CAT HOVERED NEARBY.
BUT AS SOON AS THE JABBERWOCKY DESCENDED UPON THEM, HE DISAPPEARED.
THE VILLAINOUS KNAVE OF HEARTS PICKED UP THE FALLEN SWORD...
...AND RAISED IT VICTORIOUSLY TO THE HEAVENS.

THE JABBERWOCKY, HAVING DECIMATED MY CLAN, MADE ITS RETREAT.
THIS BURNT, CRUSHED HAT...
...WAS ALL THAT WAS LEFT WHERE MY BRETHREN ONCE STOOD.

READ THIS WAY

HATTER?
HATTER!!

DID YOU HEAR THAT?
I'M CERTAIN I HEARD SOMETHING.
I'M FINE. JUST FINE... REALLY.
ARE YOU?
VOICES?
RED KNIGHTS!

READ THIS WAY

タタ
タ
タタタタ
タ
ダダダ
ダダダ
ザザッ
ザッ
ザ
ダダ
ダ

THE WHITE QUEEN'S CASTLE IS JUST BEYOND.
GO SOUTH TO GRAMPAS BLUFFS.

READ THIS WAY
チャッ
スタッ
?
JUMP ON THE HAT. NOW!!
くる
くる
DOWNAL WYTH BLUDDY BEHG HID!!

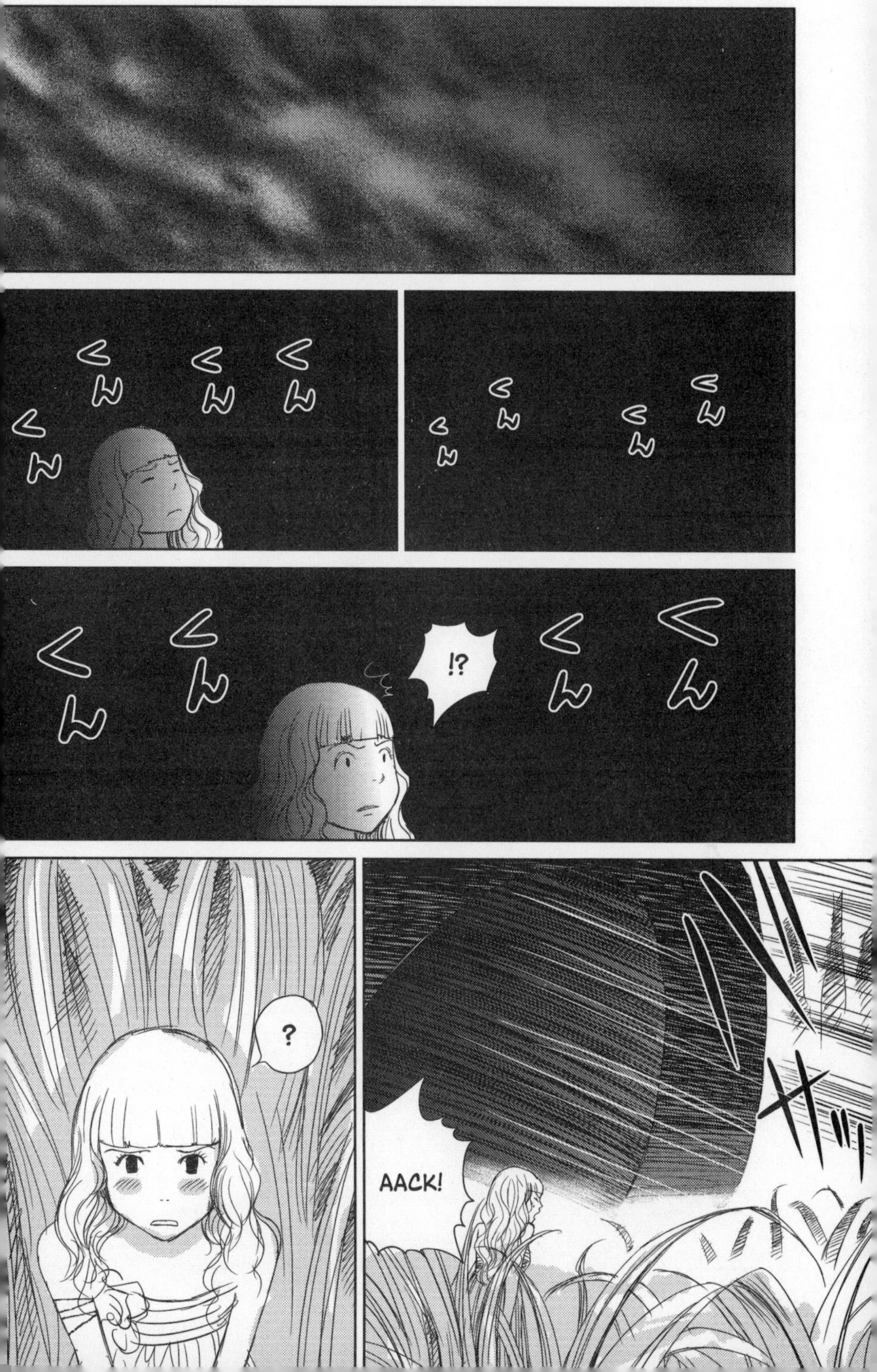
!?
?
AACK!

!!
THE HATTER TRUSTED YOU!!
YOU TURNCOAT! YOU WERE SUPPOSED TO LEAD THEM AWAY!
THEY HAVE MY WIFE AND PUPS.

WHAT'S YOUR NAME?
BAYARD.
SIT!
?
SIT!!
WOULD YOUR NAME BE "ALICE" BY ANY CHANCE?
YES, BUT I'M NOT THAT ONE.
THE HATTER WOULD NOT HAVE GIVEN HIMSELF UP FOR JUST ANY ALICE.
WHERE DID THEY TAKE HIM?
TO THE RED QUEEN'S CASTLE AT SALAZEN GRUM.

WE'RE GOING TO GO RESCUE HIM.
THE FRABJOUS DAY IS ALMOST UPON US. YOU MUST PREPARE TO MEET THE JABBERWOCKY.
I DON'T CARE. HE WOULDN'T BE THERE IF IT WEREN'T FOR ME.
THAT IS NOT FORETOLD ...
I HAVE HAD QUITE ENOUGH!
SINCE THE MOMENT I FELL DOWN THAT RABBIT HOLE, I'VE BEEN TOLD WHAT I MUST DO AND WHO I MUST BE.
I'VE BEEN SHRUNK, STRETCHED, SCRATCHED, AND STUFFED INTO A TEAPOT!

I'VE BEEN ACCUSED OF BEING ALICE AND OF NOT BEING ALICE.
BUT THIS IS MY DREAM! I'LL DECIDE HOW IT GOES FROM HERE.
IF YOU DIVERGE FROM THE PATH...
I MAKE THE PATH!

TAKE ME TO SALAZEN GRUM!
AND DON'T FORGET THE HAT!
スタッ
タタッ

タタッ
タタッ

READ THIS WAY
SALAZEN GRUM: CASTLE OF THE RED QUEEN
THERE'S ONLY ONE WAY ACROSS.

グニャ
トン
YEEUCK
...
ハァ
ハァ
BAYARD!
THE HAT!

READ THIS WAY

くるくるくる
ぶん
ドスッ
ワオーーッ
タタッ
あははは
あははは
コーーー

SHHHH. I WANT TO HELP YOU.
EEKEEK!

READ THIS WAY

WHERE'S MY BALL? PAGE!
ドキッ
ササササ
スッ
WELL!
IF IT ISN'T THE WRONG ALICE.
WHAT BRINGS YOU HERE?
I'VE COME FOR TWO REASONS.
THAT'S FOR DRAGGING ME DOWN HERE AGAINST MY WILL!

YOU DIDN'T HAVE TO HIT ME! NOW THERE'S GOING TO BE A BRUISE.
IS THERE ??
NO.
WHAT'S THE OTHER REASON?
I'M GOING TO RESCUE THE HATTER.
YOU'RE NOT RESCUING ANYONE BEING THE SIZE OF A GERBIL.
DO YOU HAVE ANY OF THAT CAKE THAT MADE ME GROW BEFORE?
UPELKUCHEN?
ACTUALLY, I MIGHT HAVE SOME LEFT.

READ THIS WAY

がさ
がさ
ざっ
NOT ALL OF IT!!
OH, NO... STOP! DON'T DO THAT!

AND WHAT IS THIS?!

6 That "A"-Something Girl

IT'S A... "WHO," YOUR MAJESTY. THIS IS... UM...
UM?
FROM UMBRADGE, YOUR MAJESTY.

I OUTGREW THEM.
WHAT HAPPENED TO YOUR GARMENTS?
I TOWER OVER EVERYONE IN UMBRADGE. THEY LAUGH AT ME.
SO I'VE COME TO YOU, YOUR MAJESTY, HOPING YOU WOULD UNDERSTAND WHAT IT'S LIKE.

MY DEAR GIRL, ANYONE WITH A HEAD THAT LARGE IS WELCOME IN MY COURT.
ゆく
ゆく
SOMEONE FIND HER SOME CLOTHES! USE THE DRAPERIES IF YOU MUST BUT CLOTHE THIS ENORMOUS GIRL!
YOU'LL BE MY NEW FAVORITE.

I NEED A PIG HERE!
I LOVE A WARM PIG BELLY FOR MY ACHING FEET.

ドキドキ
ドキドキ
WHERE ARE MY FATBOYS?
YOU MUST MEET THEM! FAT-BOOOOYS!
ドキ
GO AWAY.

THERE THEY ARE! AREN'T THEY ADORABLE?
AND THEY HAVE THE ODDEST WAY OF SPEAKING. SPEAK, BOYS. AMUSE US.

SPEAK!
IS THAT BEING ...?
NO, IT ISN'T.
NOT A BIT.

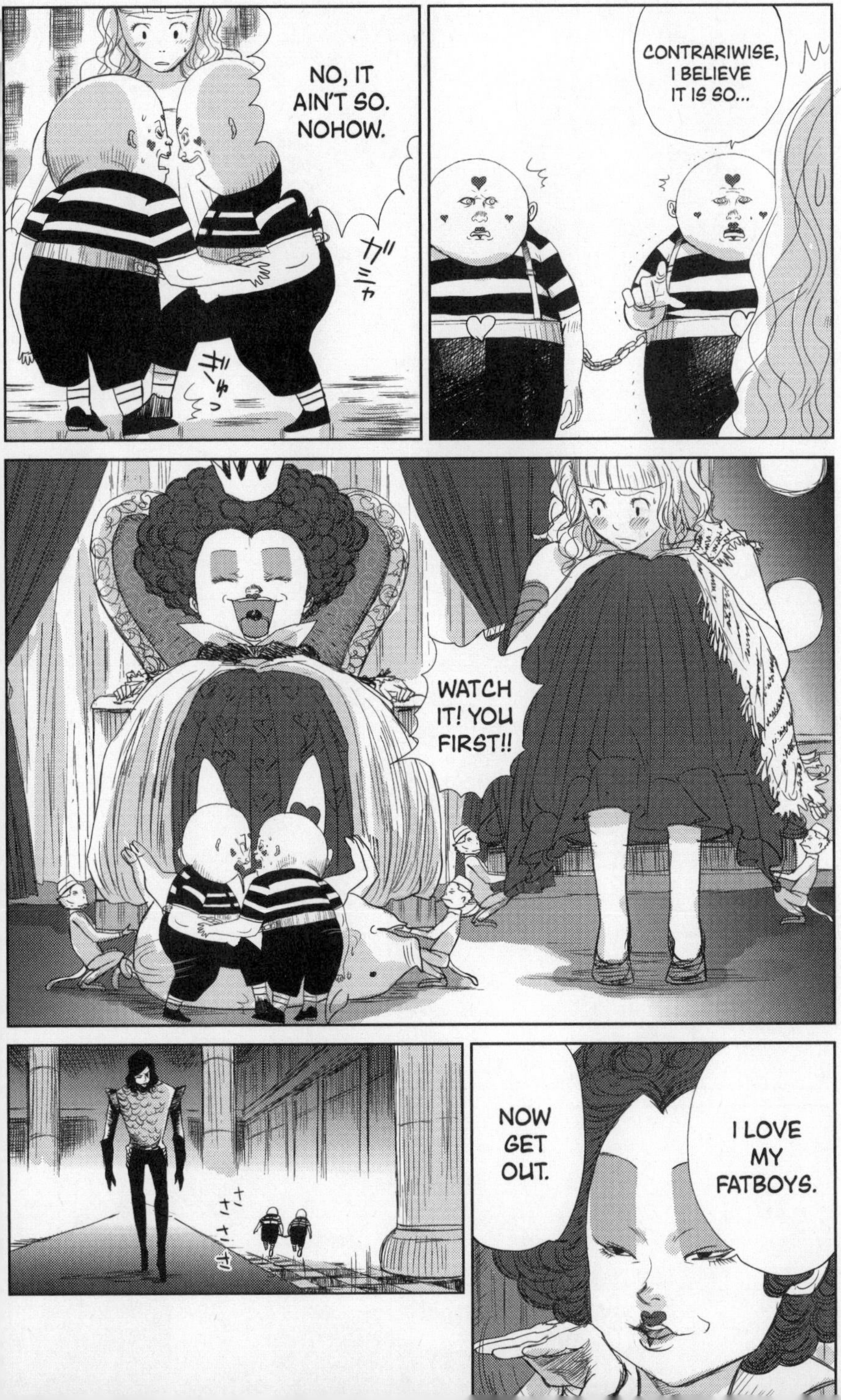
NO, IT AIN'T SO. NOHOW.
ガシャ
ガシャ
CONTRARIWISE, I BELIEVE IT IS SO...
WATCH IT! YOU FIRST!!
NOW GET OUT.
I LOVE MY FATBOYS.

はあああああ
....
.........!
THERE YOU ARE, STAYNE. ANY LUCK WITH THE PRISONER?
HE'S STUBBORN.
YOU'RE TOO SOFT. BRING HIM!
AND WHO IS THIS LOVELY CREATURE?
UM, MY NEW FAVORITE.

DOES SHE HAVE A NAME?
UM.
YES? HER NAME?
IT'S UM!
I BELIEVE YOUR NAME HAS SLIPPED THE QUEEN'S MIND.
カチン

HER NAME IS UM, YOU DOLT!
FROM UMBRADGE.
ILOSOVIC STAYNE, AT YOUR SERVICE.

!!!
ジャラ
しょぼん
グイッ
WE KNOW ALICE HAS RETURNED TO UNDERLAND. DO YOU KNOW WHERE SHE IS?

READ THIS WAY

DREADFULLY SORRY. I'VE BEEN CONSIDERING THINGS THAT BEGIN WITH THE LETTER "M."
MORON, MUTINY, MURDER, MALICE...
WE'RE LOOKING FOR AN "A" WORD NOW.

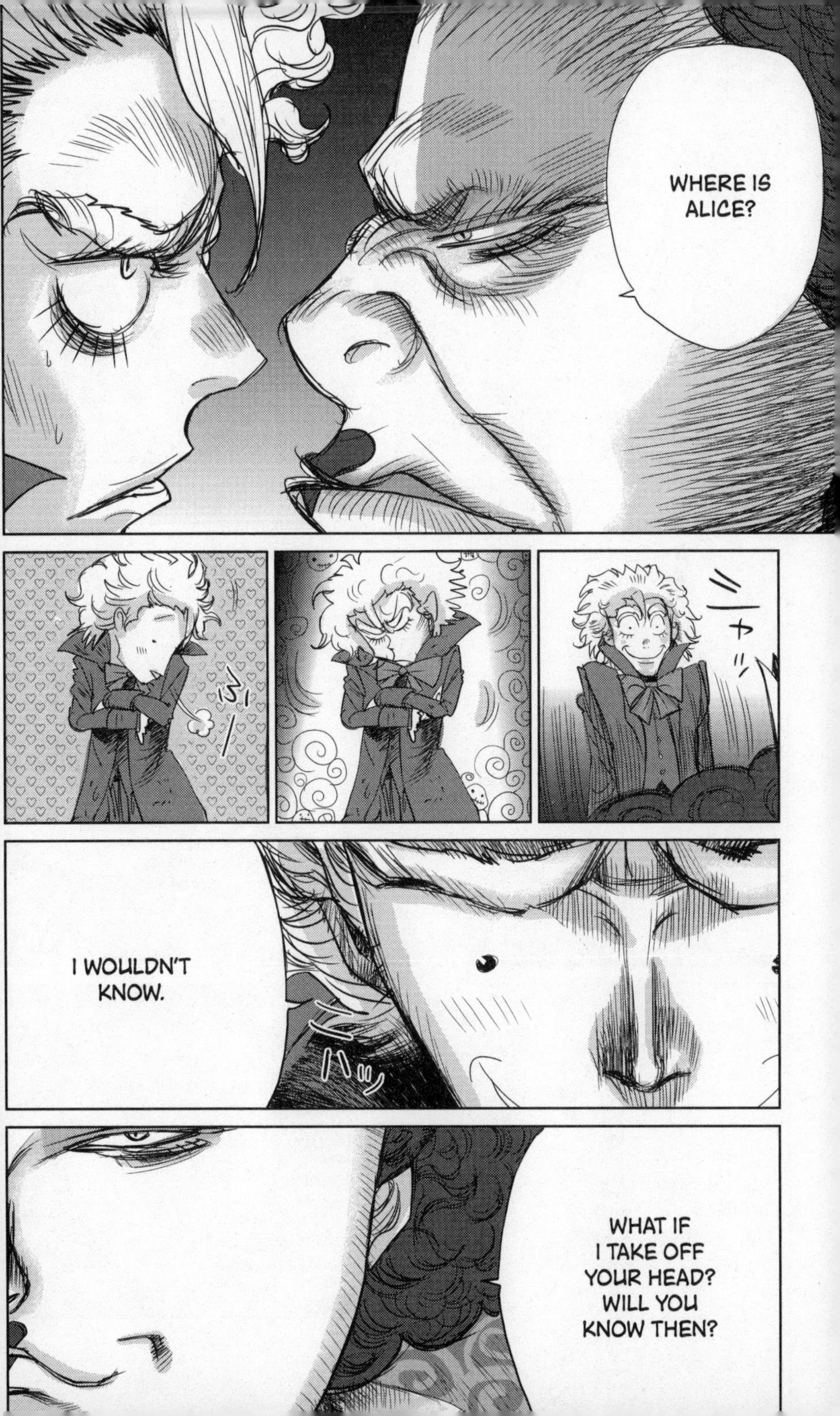
WHERE IS ALICE?
ふー
ニヤッ
I WOULDN'T KNOW.
ニハッ
WHAT IF I TAKE OFF YOUR HEAD? WILL YOU KNOW THEN?

HEE
HEE HA HA HA HA HA HA!
STOP THAT!
ドキッ

MY, WHAT A REGRET-TABLY LARGE HEAD YOU HAVE.
I SHOULD VERY MUCH LIKE TO HAT IT.
HAT IT?
YES, I USED TO HAT THE WHITE QUEEN, YOU KNOW, BUT THERE WASN'T VERY MUCH FOR ME TO WORK WITH, POOR DEAR. HER HEAD IS SO SMALL.
IT'S TINY.
A PIMPLE OF A HEAD...
BUT THIS... WHAT I COULD DO WITH THIS MONUMENT, THIS ORB...?
WHAT COULD YOU DO?

ジャラ
ジャラ
UNBIND HIM, STAYNE!
HOW CAN HE WORK IF HIS HANDS ARE BOUND?
ガチャ
ガチャ
SHALL IT BE A BONNET OR A BOATER?
OR SOMETHING FOR THE BOUDOIR?
A CLOCHE! DUNCE CAP!
A DEATH CAP, COIF, OR EVEN A SNOOD!

BARBOOSH ...?
OR PUGREE ...?
HATTER!!
I'M FINE. I'M FINE.
LEAVE US.
SHOO, SHOO!

READ THIS WAY

コッ
コッ
コッ
AAAAAH!!!
ガッ
I LIKE YOU, UM.
I LIKE THEM... LARGE.
ぬっ

ドカッ
GET AWAY FROM ME!
ダッ
タッ タッ
タッ タッ

AH, BAYARD. HAS SOMETHING HAPPENED?
よろよろ
フララ

ALICE HAS RETURNED TO UNDERLAND.
WHERE IS SHE NOW?
IN SALAZEN GRUM. FORGIVE ME, I ALLOWED HER TO DIVERT FROM HER DESTINED PATH.
BUT THAT IS EXACTLY WHERE SHE WILL FIND THE VORPAL SWORD. WE HAVE OUR CHAMPION!
REST NOW. YOU'VE DONE WELL.

READ THIS WAY

CASTLE OF THE RED QUEEN
ザッ
キョロ キョロ
FOUND IT!
ザッ

WITHOUT THE JABBERWOCKY, MY SISTER'S FOLLOWERS WILL SURELY RISE AGAINST ME.
YOU MUST FIND ALICE, STAYNE!
WHY DO THEY ADORE HER AND NOT ME?
MY UGLY LITTLE SISTER ...
I CANNOT FATHOM IT. YOU ARE FAR SUPERIOR IN ALL WAYS.
I KNOW. BUT MIRANA CAN MAKE ANYONE FALL IN LOVE WITH HER. MEN, WOMEN, EVEN THE FURNITURE...

READ THIS WAY

EVEN THE KING.
I HAD TO DO IT. HE WOULD HAVE LEFT ME.
MAJESTY, ISN'T IT BETTER TO BE FEARED THAN LOVED?
I'M NOT CERTAIN ANYMORE.
OH, LET HER HAVE THE RABBLE!
I DON'T NEED THEM. I HAVE YOU.

I DO HAVE YOU, DON'T I, STAYNE?
ウルウル
ウルウル

7 The Vorpal Sword

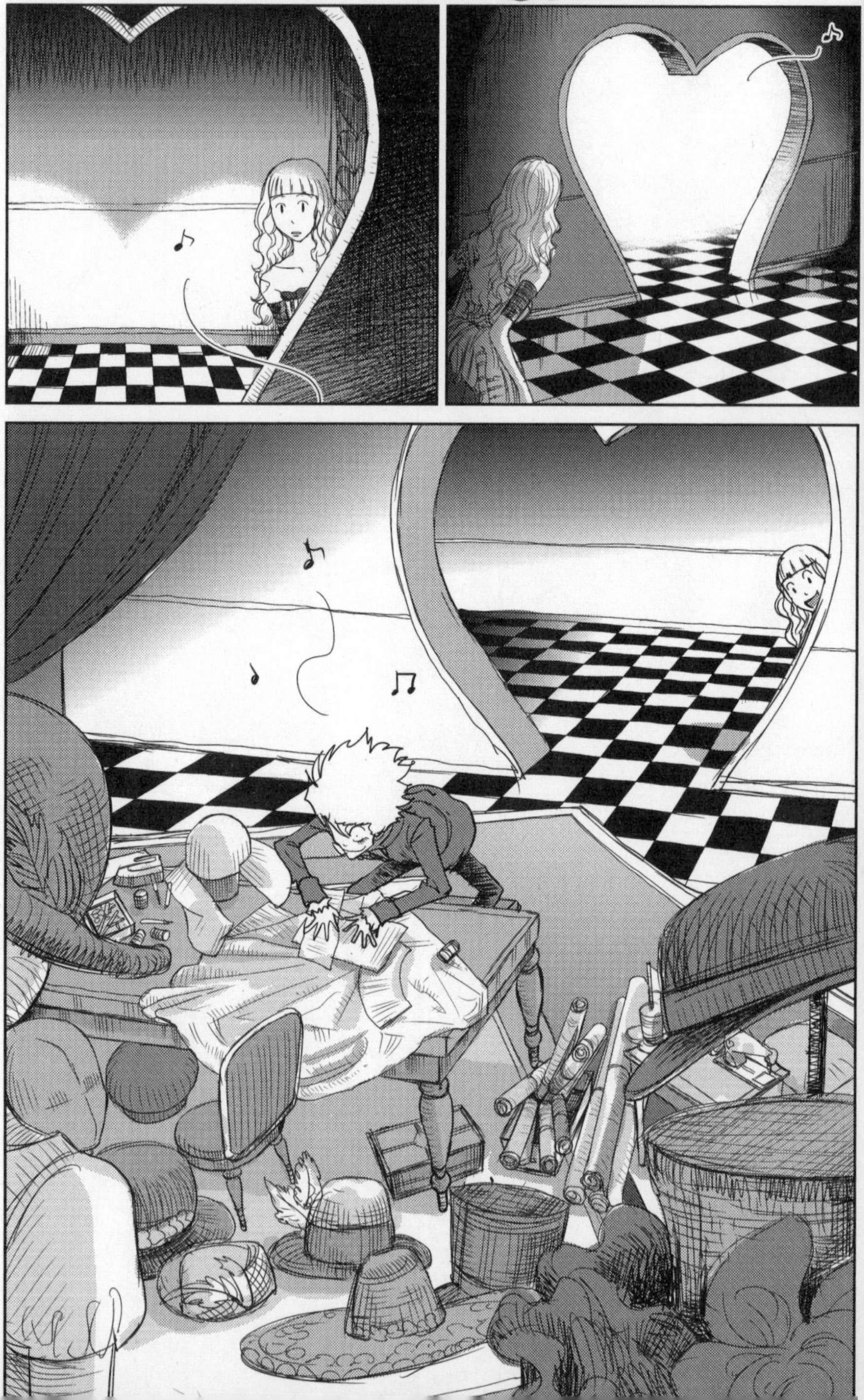

THEY'RE WONDER-FUL! YOU MUST LET ME TRY ONE ON!
あははははは

IT'S GOOD TO BE WORKING AT MY TRADE AGAIN.
IT'S JUST A PITY YOU HAD TO MAKE THEM FOR HER.
しゅぼ～ん
WHAT'S THE HATTER WITH ME? THE HATTER. MMM... MA... MAHA... MWA-HAHAHAHA!
う～
プルプル
カクカク
カクカク
シャッ
チョキ
チョキ
チョキ
チョキ
STOP! STOP!

HATTER!!
HAVE I GONE MAD?

I'M AFRAID SO. YOU'RE ENTIRELY BONKERS.
BUT I'LL TELL YOU A SECRET...
ALL THE BEST PEOPLE ARE.

OH, LOOK! HERE'S ANOTHER ONE.
がさ がさ
THAT'S BETTER. YOU LOOK YOURSELF AGAIN.
ぎゅっ

HAT MAN! WHERE ARE MY HATS?
I AM NOT A PATIENT MONARCH!
I'M TOLD SHE KEEPS THE VORPAL SWORD HIDDEN IN THE CASTLE. FIND IT, ALICE. TAKE IT TO THE WHITE QUEEN. HELP US MAKE THE WORLD RIGHT AGAIN!
WE'LL GO TO THE WHITE QUEEN TOGETHER.

WHY IS
IT YOU'RE
ALWAYS TOO
SMALL OR
TOO TALL?

READ THIS WAY

TWEEDLES!
HOWDOYEDO AGAIN.
WHERE'S ...?
キョロ
HOW IS IT YOU'RE BEING SO GREAT-BIG?
SHE AIN'T GREAT-BIG. THIS IS HOW SHE NORMAL IS.
キョロ
I'M CERTAIN SHE WAS SMALLER WHEN WE MET.

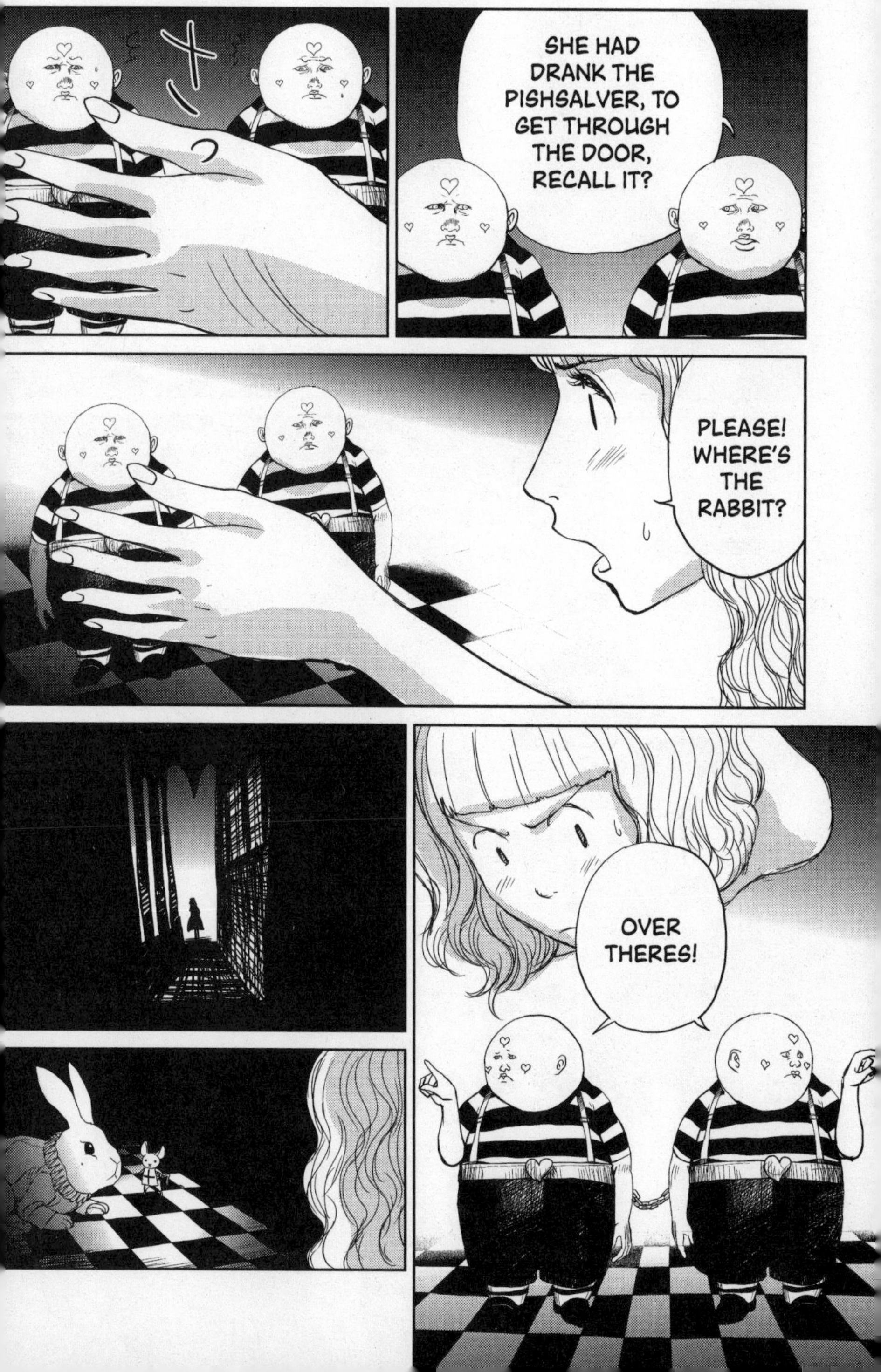
SHE HAD DRANK THE PISHSALVER, TO GET THROUGH THE DOOR, RECALL IT?
PLEASE! WHERE'S THE RABBIT?
OVER THERES!

WHAT ARE YOU DOING HERE?
I'M RESCUING THE HATTER.
I'M RESCUING THE HATTER. BUT YOU CAN HELP. HE TOLD ME THAT THE VORPAL SWORD IS HIDDEN IN THE CASTLE.
THAT MEANS SOMEONE MUST HAVE SEEN IT... A FOOTFROG, A CHAMBER MOUSE, A PIGSTOOL... SOMEONE!
ASK THEM ALL! GO!

I DON'T TAKE ORDERS FROM BIG, CLUMSY, GALUMPH-ING...
SHOO!
スタタタ

READ THIS WAY

WHAT IS IT, MCTWISP?
I KNOW WHERE THE SWORD IS.
WHY DIDN'T YOU SAY SO?
YOU'LL HIT ME AGAIN.
I WON'T HIT YOU!

THE SWORD'S HIDDEN INSIDE.
ガッちゃ
ギィイイイ
モァ
I KNOW THAT SMELL.
そ〜

...
I'M NOT GOING IN THERE! LOOK AT WHAT THAT THING DID TO MY ARM!

DEAR, OH, DEAR! WHY HAVEN'T YOU MENTIONED THIS??
IT WASN'T THIS BAD BEFORE.

READ THIS WAY

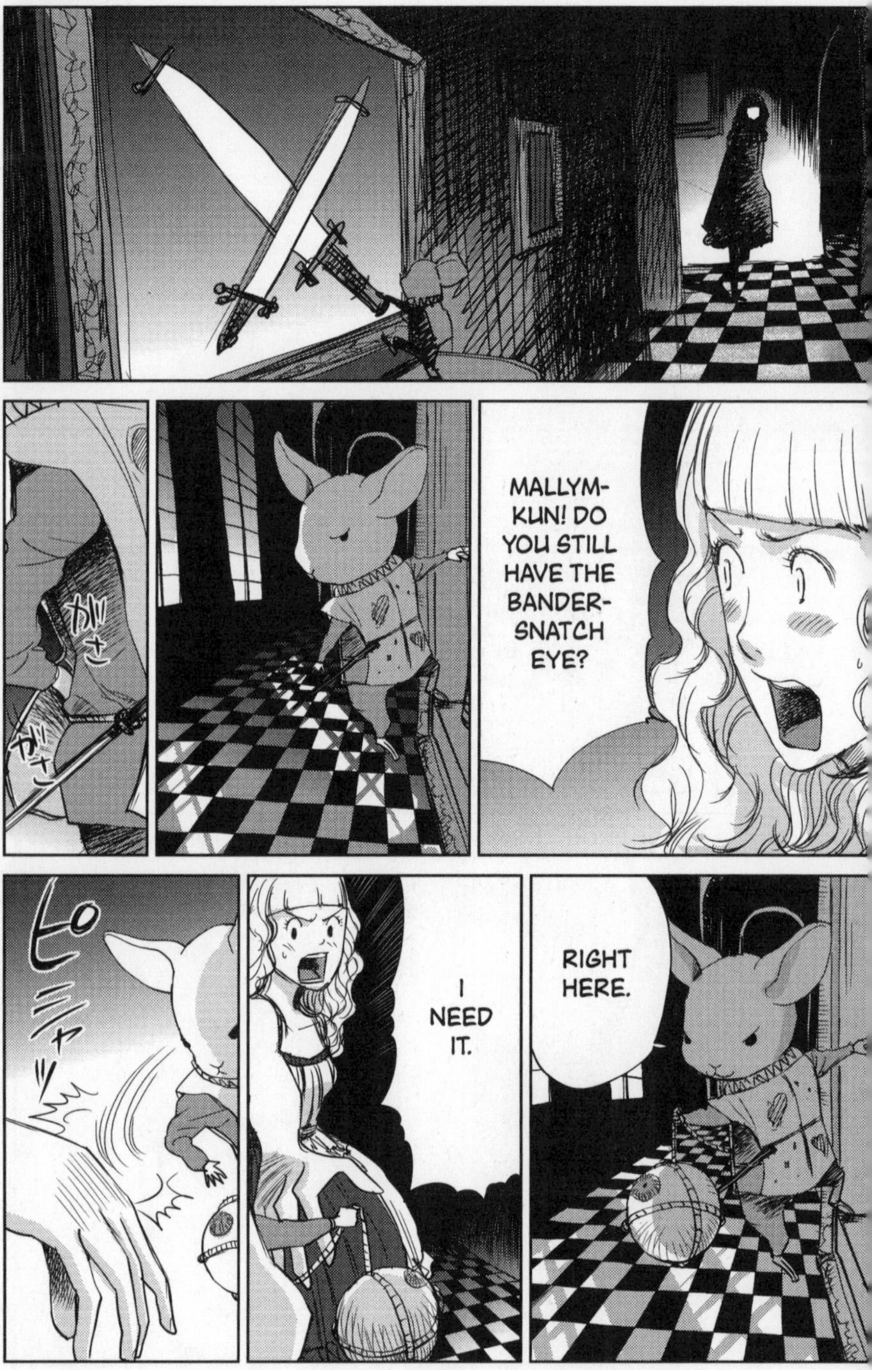
MALLYM-KUN! DO YOU STILL HAVE THE BANDER-SNATCH EYE?
RIGHT HERE.
I NEED IT.

GET YOUR OWN!
I NEED THAT EYE, MALLY.
COME AND GET IT.
TEE HEE
HEE HEE HEE
RIGHT.

ガチャッ
しゅっ
こつん
ズッ
HAVE AT YOU!
シュッ
スカッ
よろ
よろ
よろ
つん
チクッ
OW!
よろ
NO, STAB-BING!
THRUST-ING NOW!
THRUST-ING LIKE THIS!

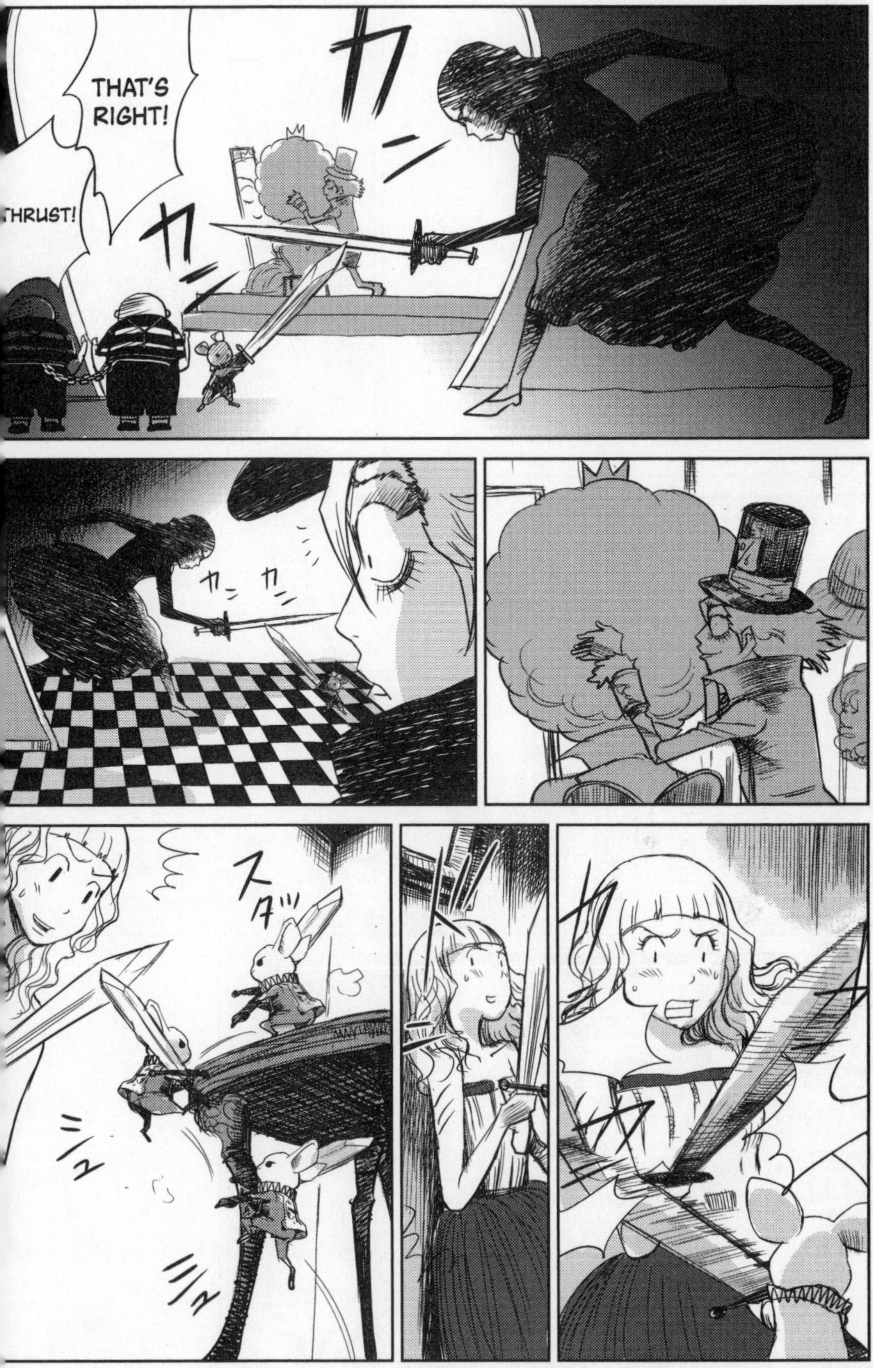

THAT'S RIGHT!
THRUST!
カン
カン
カン カン
スダッ
シュ
シュ

ニャッ
シュッ
ガッ

スタタッ
I HAVE YOUR EYE.
ウオオオオオオ
オオオオオオ

バサッ
がちゃがちゃ
NNNG!
ズキン
YOU ARE STUNNING IN THAT HAT!
YOUR MAJESTY HAS NEVER LOOKED BETTER.

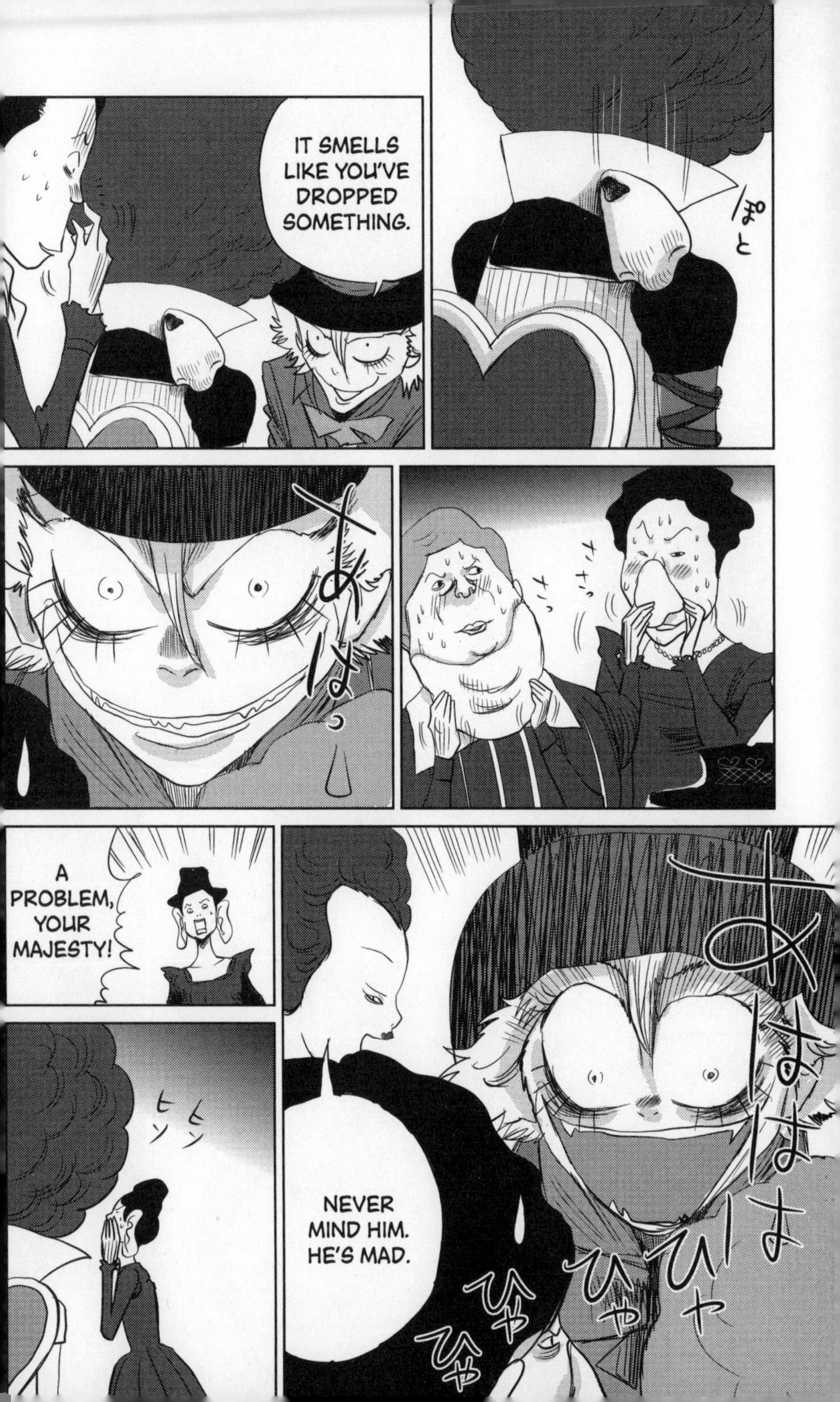

ぽと
IT SMELLS LIKE YOU'VE DROPPED SOMETHING.
NEVER MIND HIM. HE'S MAD.
A PROBLEM, YOUR MAJESTY!
ヒソヒソ

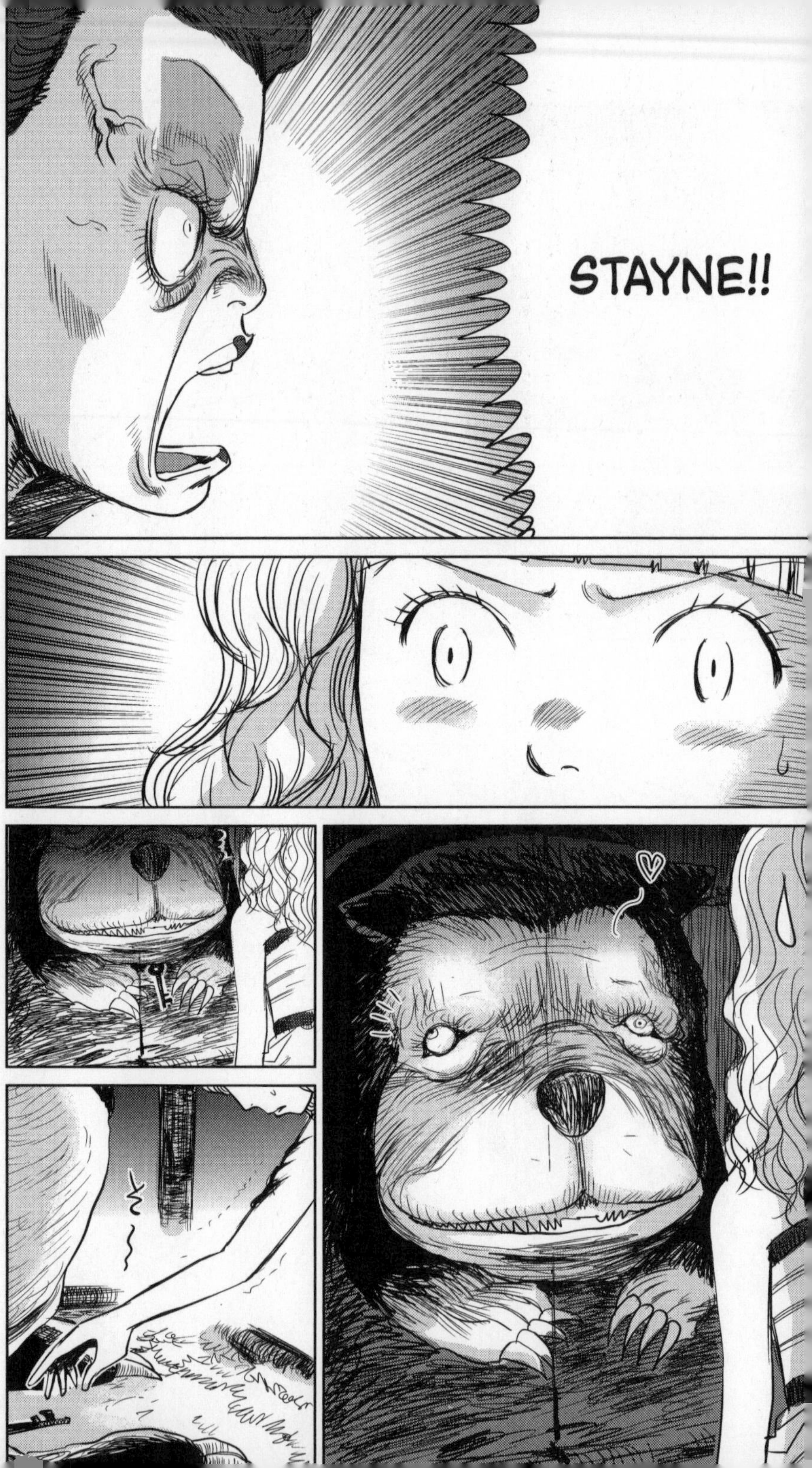
STAYNE!!

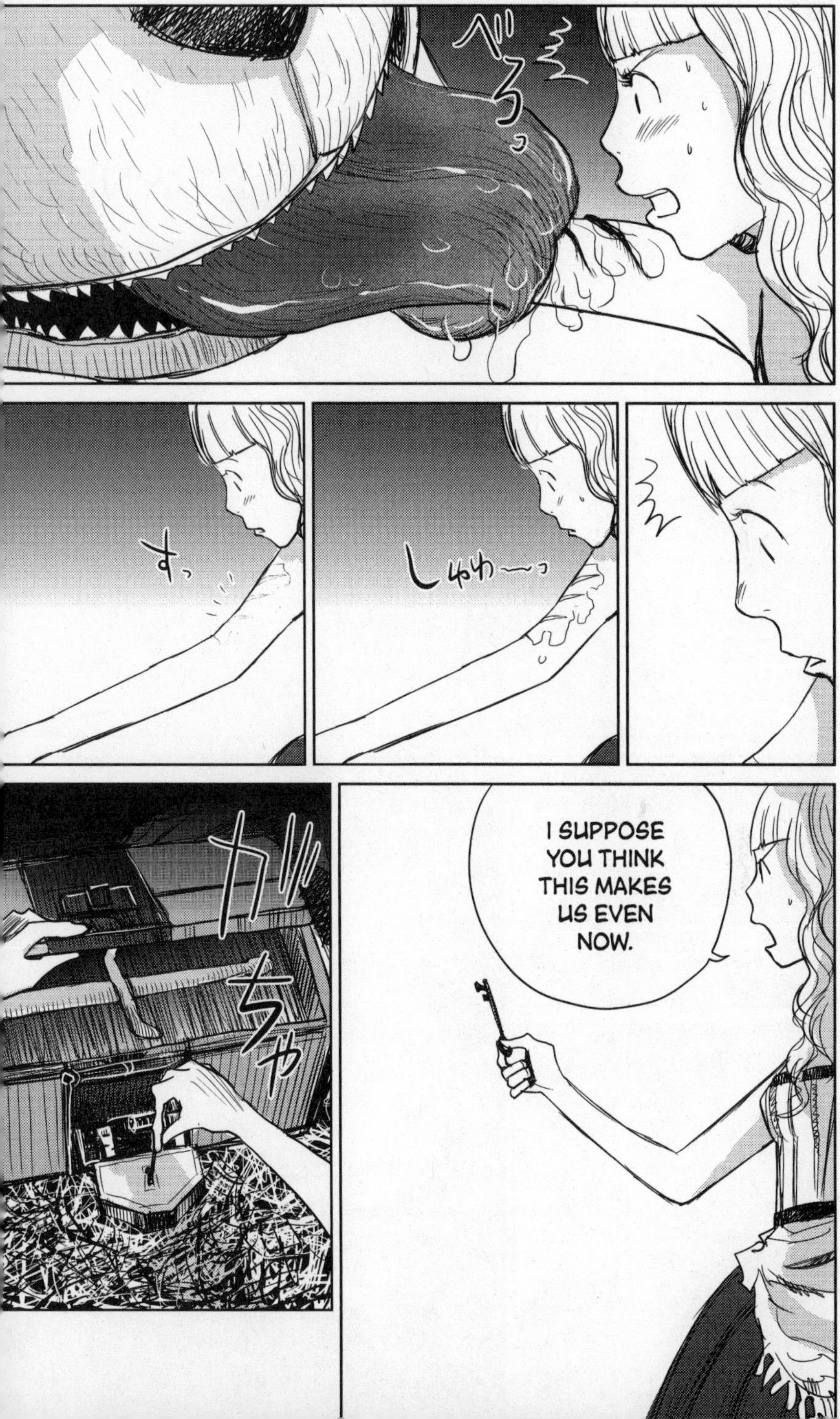
べろっ
すっ
しゅわ〜っ
ガちゃ
I SUPPOSE YOU THINK THIS MAKES US EVEN NOW.

UM FORCED HERSELF ON ME.
I TOLD HER THAT MY HEART BELONGS TO YOU. BUT SHE'S OBSESSED WITH ME.
OFF WITH HER HEAD!

Disney

Alice in Wonderland

8 Run!

READ THIS WAY
カチャ
カチャ
がちゃ
がちゃ
ぐにゃ
STAND BACK, MALLYM-KUN.

READ THIS WAY
HOW'S THIS FOR "MUCHNESS"?
STOP! IT MUSTN'T BE USED FOR ANYTHING BUT...

ザザッ!!

ARREST THAT GIRL FOR UNLAWFUL SEDUCTION.
HATTER!

カン
カン
カン
カン
ス
ズス
ブス
ブス

WE REALLY MUSTN'T USE THE SWORD!
TAKE IT TO THE WHITE QUEEN!
I'M NOT LEAVING WITHOUT YOU!!
GET OUT OF HERE, ALICE!
ALICE...?

READ THIS WAY

ALICE! GO! NOW!
SEIZE HER!

ダッ ダッ
タッ
タッ
ダッ
チャッ

ALICE. OF COURSE! WHY DIDN'T I SEE IT?
WELL, IT HAS BEEN A LONG TIME.
AND YOU WERE SUCH A LITTLE TYKE THEN.

READ THIS WAY

GIVE ME THE SWORD.
STAY BACK!
THE QUEEN WILL BE SO PLEASED. SHE'LL TAKE GREAT PLEASURE IN TAKING OFF YOUR HEAD. I BELIEVE SHE WANTS TO DO THE DEED HERSELF.

ガオオオオオ

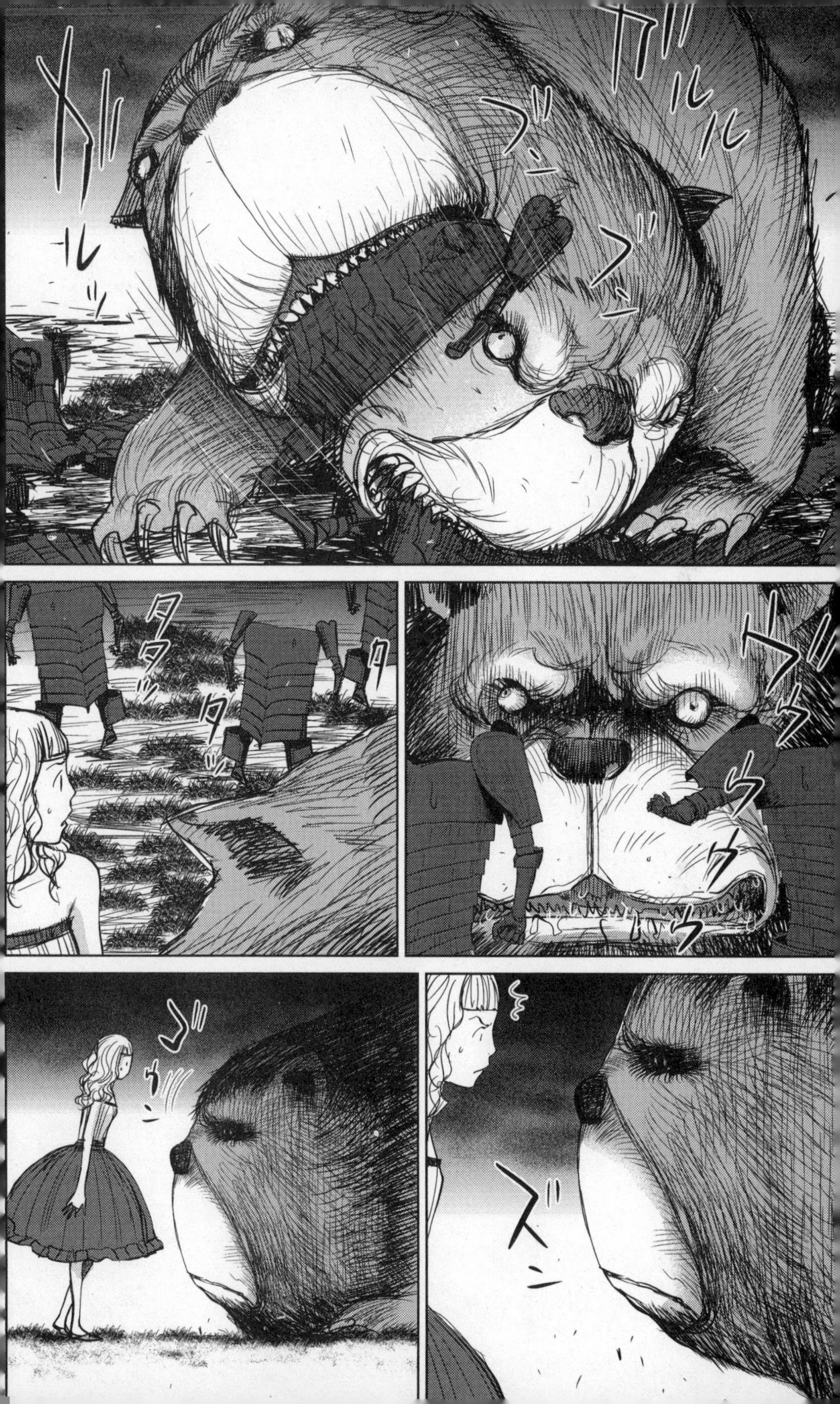
ガルルル
ブー
ブー
タ
タタッ
タッ
ヴゥゥゥゥ
ズー

スタッ
DOWNAL WYTH BLUDDY BEHG HID!!

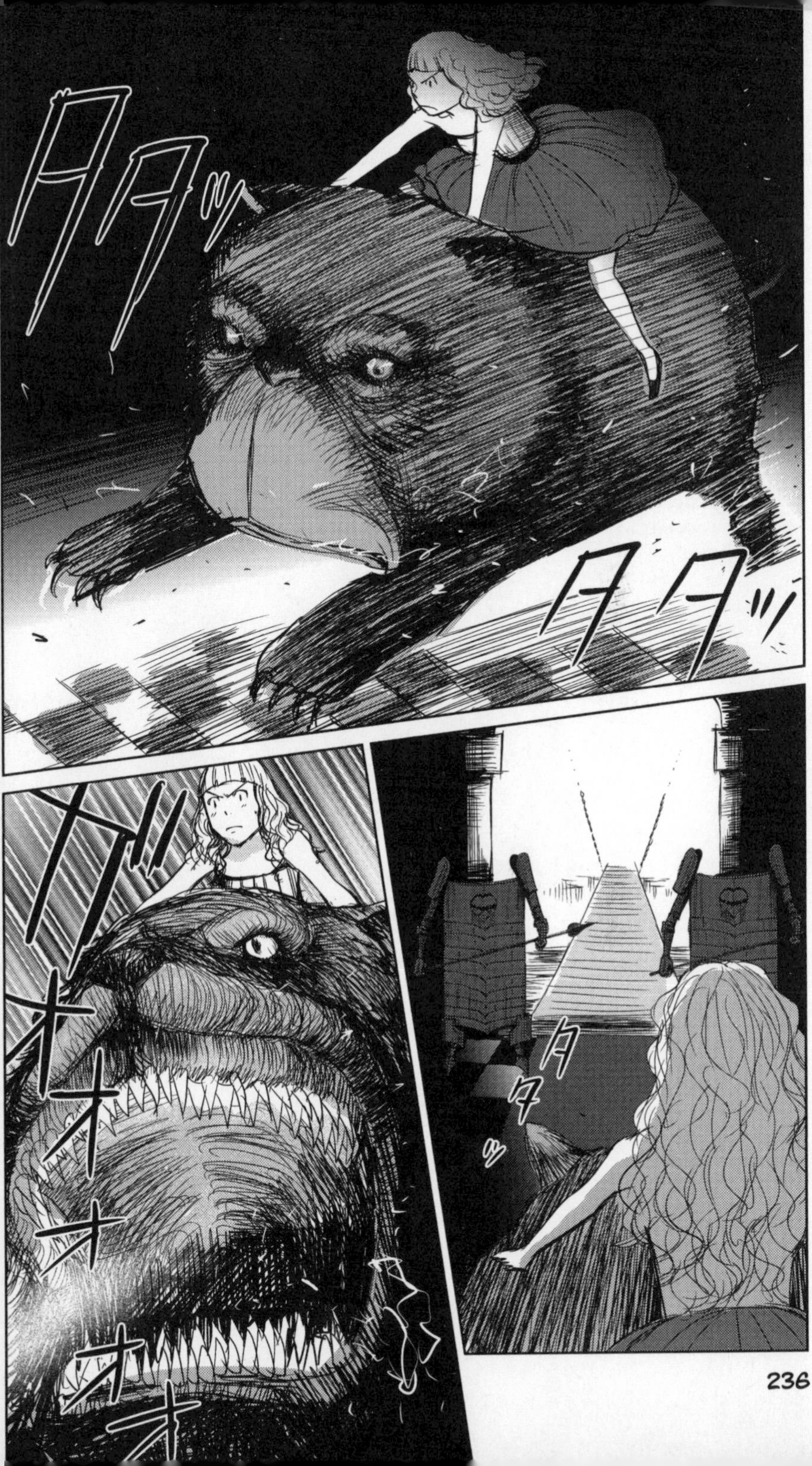
タタッ
タタッ
タタッ

ALICE, YOU'RE ALIVE!
BAYARD! TO MARMO-REAL!

ごうごう

SHH

WELCOME TO MARMOREAL.

READ THIS WAY

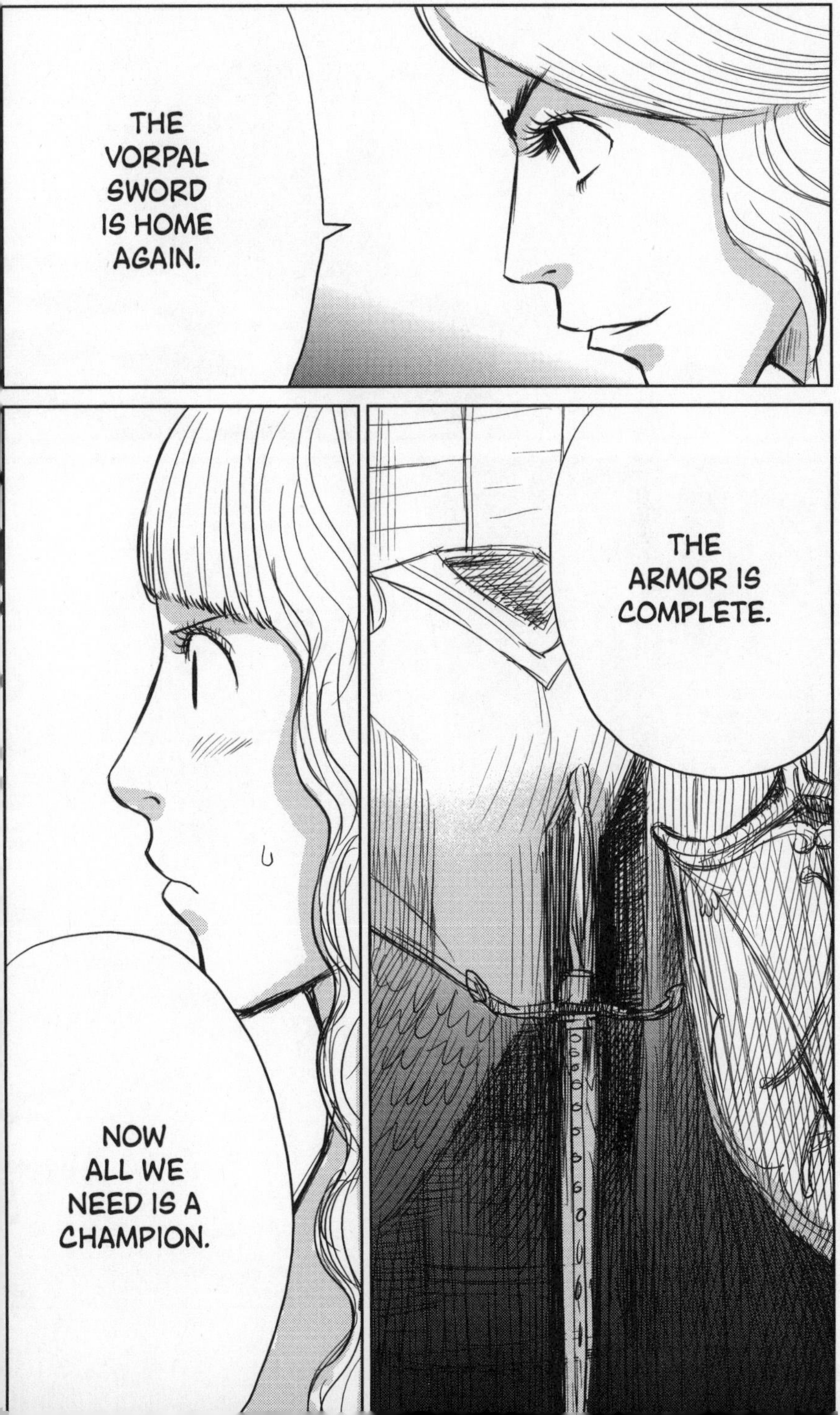
THE VORPAL SWORD IS HOME AGAIN.
THE ARMOR IS COMPLETE.
NOW ALL WE NEED IS A CHAMPION.

READ THIS WAY
YOU'RE A LITTLE TALLER THAN I THOUGHT YOU'D BE.
BLAME IT ON TOO MUCH UPELKUCHEN.

COME WITH ME.

Disney

Alice in Wonderland

9 Public Execution

READ THIS WAY

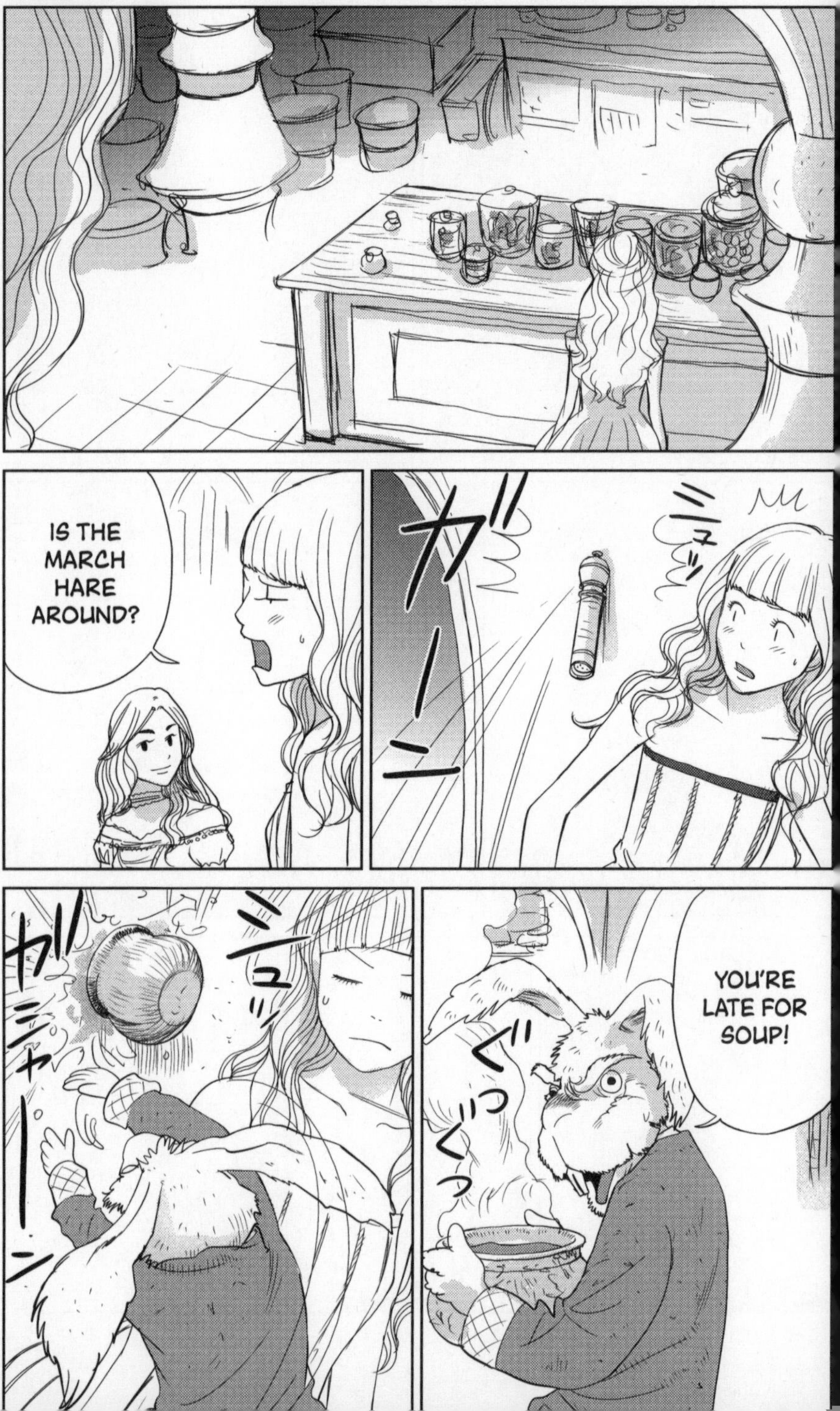

ガーン
ミュッ
IS THE MARCH HARE AROUND?
YOU'RE LATE FOR SOUP!
ぐつぐつ
シュッ
ガシャーン

べちゃ
ぺろっ
COULD USE SALT.
シュッ
サッ サッ
ぺろっ
ぐっ

...A PINCH OF WORMFAT ...
PISHSALVER, LET ME THINK. TWO CUPS GRAPE JUICE...
MY MOTHER TAUGHT ME HOW TO CONCOCT ALL THE MEDICINAL CURES AND TRANS-FORMATIONAL POTIONS.
ONE TEASPOON OF VANILLA...
MY SISTER PREFERRED TO STUDY "DOMINION OVER LIVING THINGS."
...URINE OF THE HORSEFLY, BUTTERED FINGERS...
TELL ME, HOW DOES SHE SEEM TO YOU?
PERFECTLY HORRID.
SHE WASN'T ALWAYS THAT WAY.
WELL, MAYBE SHE WAS.

AND HER HEAD?
BULBOUS, BLOATED, LIKE A BLIMP.
I THINK SHE MAY HAVE SOME KIND OF GROWTH IN THERE, SOMETHING PRESSING ON HER BRAIN.
...THREE COINS FROM A DEAD MAN'S POCKET, TWO TABLESPOONS OF WISHFUL THINKING...
YOU CAN'T IMAGINE THE THINGS THAT GO ON IN THAT PLACE.
OH, YES, I CAN.
BUT WHEN A CHAMPION APPEARS TO SLAY THE JABBERWOCKY, THE PEOPLE WILL RISE AGAINST HER.
BLOW.
THAT SHOULD DO IT.

シュウウウ
ゴク
FEEL BETTER?
MUCH. THANK YOU.
THERE'S SOMEONE HERE WHO WOULD LIKE TO SPEAK WITH YOU.
CASTLE OF THE RED QUEEN

MAJESTY, ALICE HAS ESCAPED.
ON THE BANDER-SNATCH.
WITH THE VORPAL SWORD.

READ THIS WAY

HOW COULD YOU LET THIS HAPPEN?!
I MAY HAVE UNDERESTIMATED HER. BUT WE HAVE HER CONSPIRATORS, THE HATTER AND A DORMOUSE.
OFF WITH THEIR HEADS!

HATTER!
HE'S 'ROUND THE BEND.
WHY ARE YOU KEEPING US HERE? WE'VE DONE NOTHING WRONG!
PITY. IT'S A BORE TO BEHEAD A MADMAN. NO WEEPING, NO BEGGING ...
BLAME YOUR HUSBAND.

HE LEFT YOU HERE TO ROT.
YOU LIE!
GRRAGH!
UNHAND ME, LUNATIC!

YOUR HEAD COMES OFF AT DAWN!
AND THAT ONE, TOO!
IT'S SUCH A SMALL, INSIGNIFICANT LITTLE HEAD. HARDLY SEEMS WORTH THE EFFORT.
WHY DON'T YOU LET HER GO? I'LL GIVE YOU AN ENTERTAINING EXECUTION. I'LL BEG. I'LL GROVEL. WEEP, ET CETERA...
I MIGHT EVEN GROVEL AT YOUR FEET!

DOWN WITH BLOODY BIG HEAD!
I WON'T TAKE YOUR PITY TO SPARE MY OWN LIFE!
HAVE A PLEASANT NIGHT.
CASTLE OF THE WHITE QUEEN
コッ
コッ

ABSOLEM?
WHO ARE YOU?

I THOUGHT WE'D SETTLED THIS.
I'M ALICE...
...BUT NOT THAT ONE.
HOW DO YOU KNOW?

YOU SAID SO YOURSELF.
I SAID YOU WERE NOT HARDLY ALICE.
BUT YOU'RE MUCH MORE HER NOW.
IN FACT, YOU'RE ALMOST ALICE.
EVEN SO, I COULDN'T SLAY THE JABBERWOCKY...
...EVEN IF MY LIFE DEPENDED UPON IT!
IT WILL.
SO I SUGGEST YOU KEEP THE VORPAL SWORD ON HAND WHEN THE FRABJOUS DAY ARRIVES.
ぴょっ

NO TOUCHING!
THERE'S NO TOUCHING!
YOU SEEM SO REAL.
SOME-TIMES, I FORGET THAT THIS IS ALL A DREAM.
STOP DOING THAT!
DUNGEON OF THE RED QUEEN

SINCE YOU WON'T BE NEEDING IT ANYMORE, WOULD YOU CONSIDER BEQUEATHING IT TO ME?
HELLO, CHESS.
I'VE ALWAYS ADMIRED THAT HAT.
I WAS LOOKING FORWARD TO SEE-ING YOU FUTTER-WACKEN.
IT'S A PITY ABOUT ALL THIS.
IT'S A FORMAL EXECUTION. I WANT TO LOOK MY BEST.

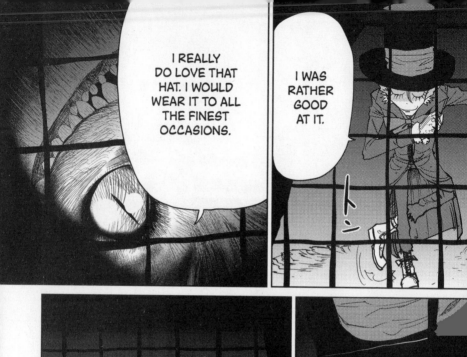

I WAS RATHER GOOD AT IT.
I REALLY DO LOVE THAT HAT. I WOULD WEAR IT TO ALL THE FINEST OCCASIONS.

ズル
キャ
ワーー
ワーー
ワーー
ワーー

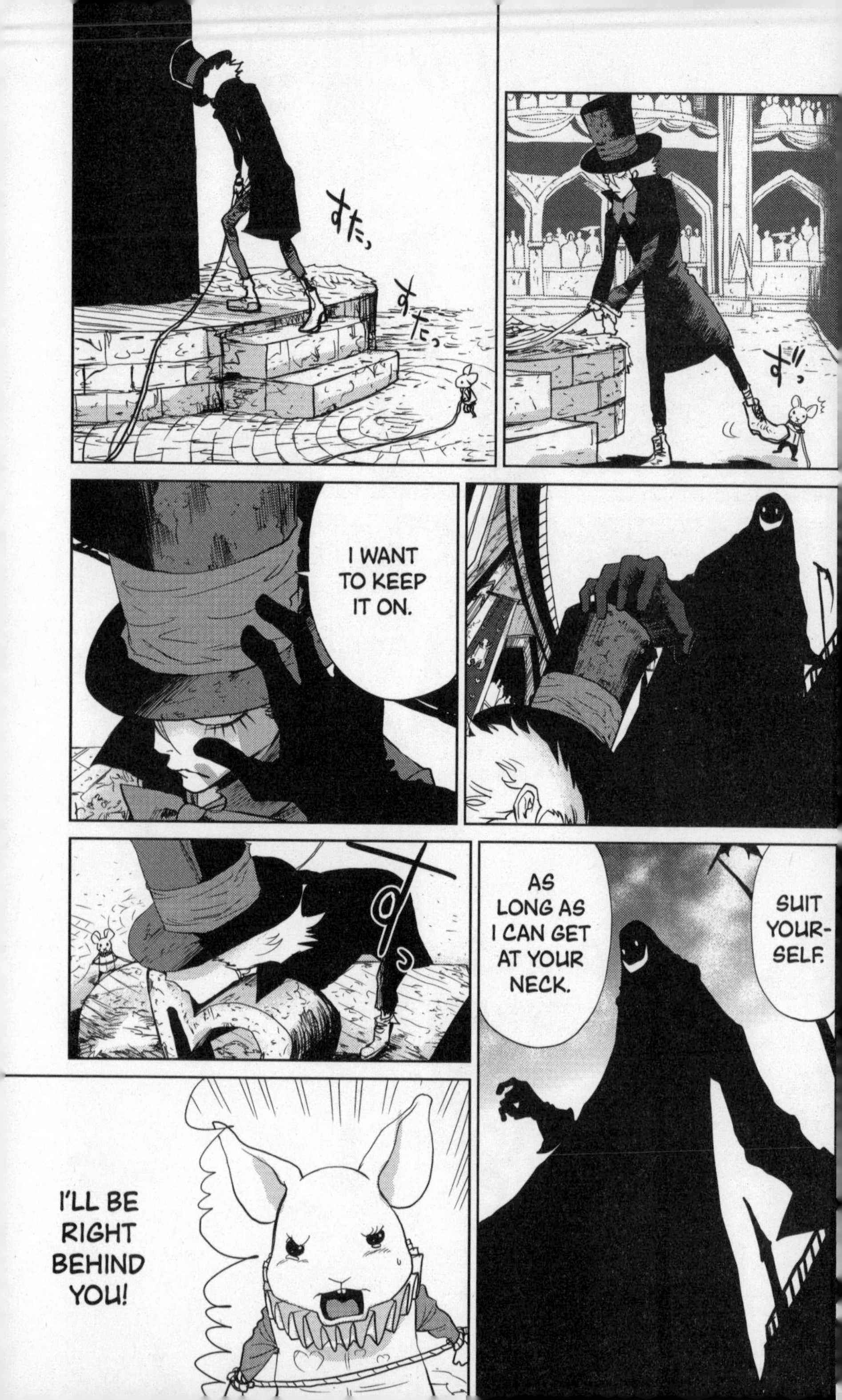
すたっ
すたっ
ずりっ
I WANT TO KEEP IT ON.
SUIT YOURSELF.
AS LONG AS I CAN GET AT YOUR NECK.
I'LL BE RIGHT BEHIND YOU!

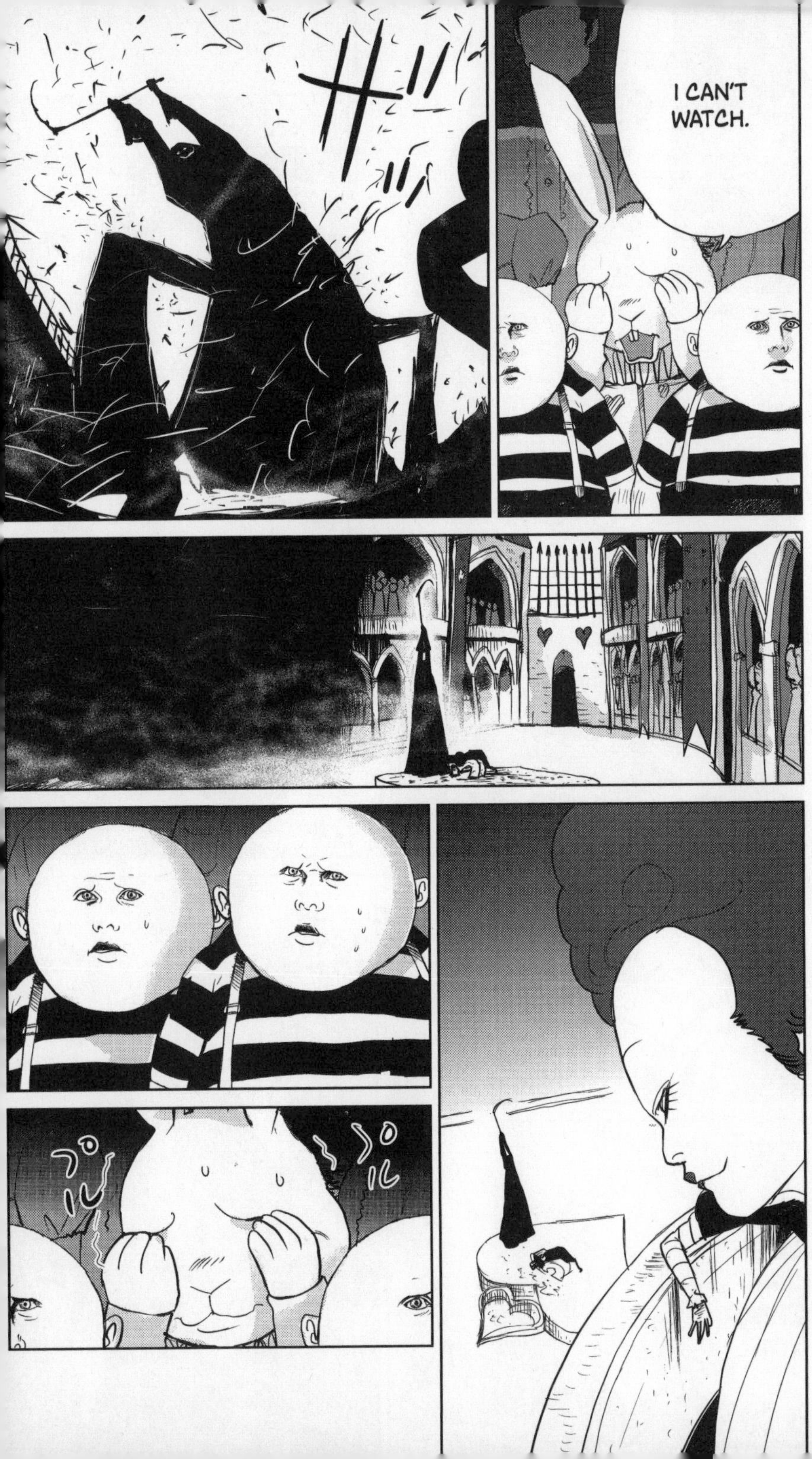
I CAN'T
WATCH.

ニヤ
IT'S GONE.
HE WAS SUCH A FINE FELLOW!
LOOK!

I CAN'T BEHEAD NOBODY IF THERE'S NO BODY!

CHESS, YOU DOG!
MAJESTY, YOUR COURTIERS ARE PLAYING YOU FOR A FOOL!

WHAT IS THAT?
I'M NOT THE ONLY ONE, MAJESTY. LOOK!
A COUN-TERFEIT NOSE?! YOU SHOULD BE ASHAMED!
ME? WHAT ABOUT THAT BIG BELLY YOU'RE SO PROUD OF?
POP!
LIARS!
CHEATS! FALSIFIERS!
OFF WITH THEIR HEADS!!

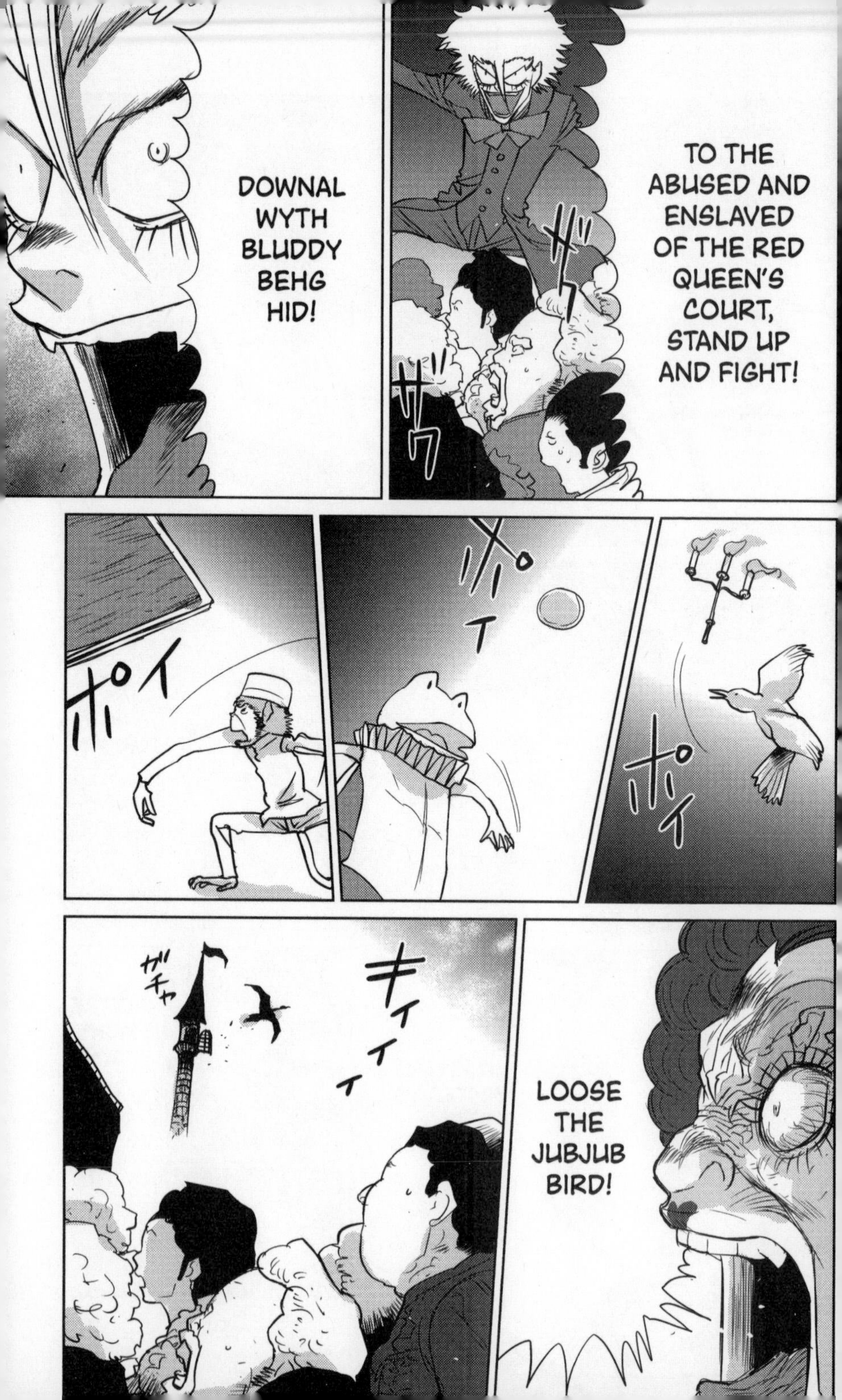
DOWNAL WYTH BLUDDY BEHG HID!
TO THE ABUSED AND ENSLAVED OF THE RED QUEEN'S COURT, STAND UP AND FIGHT!
ポイ
ポイ
ポイ
ガチャ
キイイイイ
LOOSE THE JUBJUB BIRD!

YOU'RE RIGHT, STAYNE.
IT IS FAR BETTER TO BE FEARED THAN LOVED.

CASTLE OF THE WHITE QUEEN
WE'RE GOING TO VISIT MY LITTLE SISTER!
PREPARE THE JABBER-WOCKY FOR BATTLE.
WHY DON'T YOU SLAY THE JABBERWOCKY YOURSELF? YOU MUST HAVE THE POWER.
I HAD HOPED TO HAVE A CHAMPION BY NOW.
IN THE HEALING ARTS...IT IS AGAINST MY VOWS TO BRING HARM TO ANY LIVING THING.

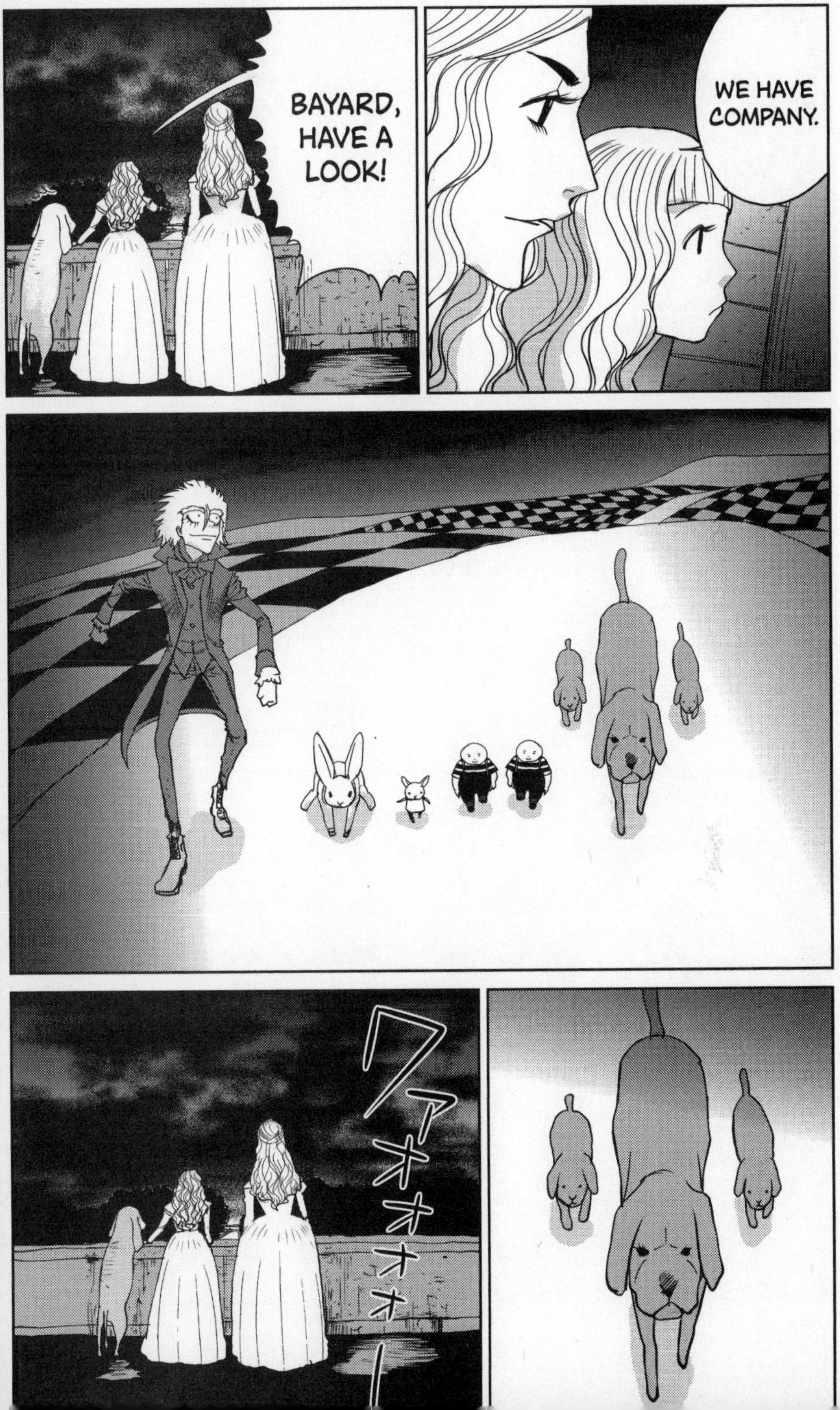
WE HAVE COMPANY.
BAYARD, HAVE A LOOK!
ワアオオオオー

DISNEY

ALICE IN WONDERLAND

10 Wonderland

READ THIS WAY

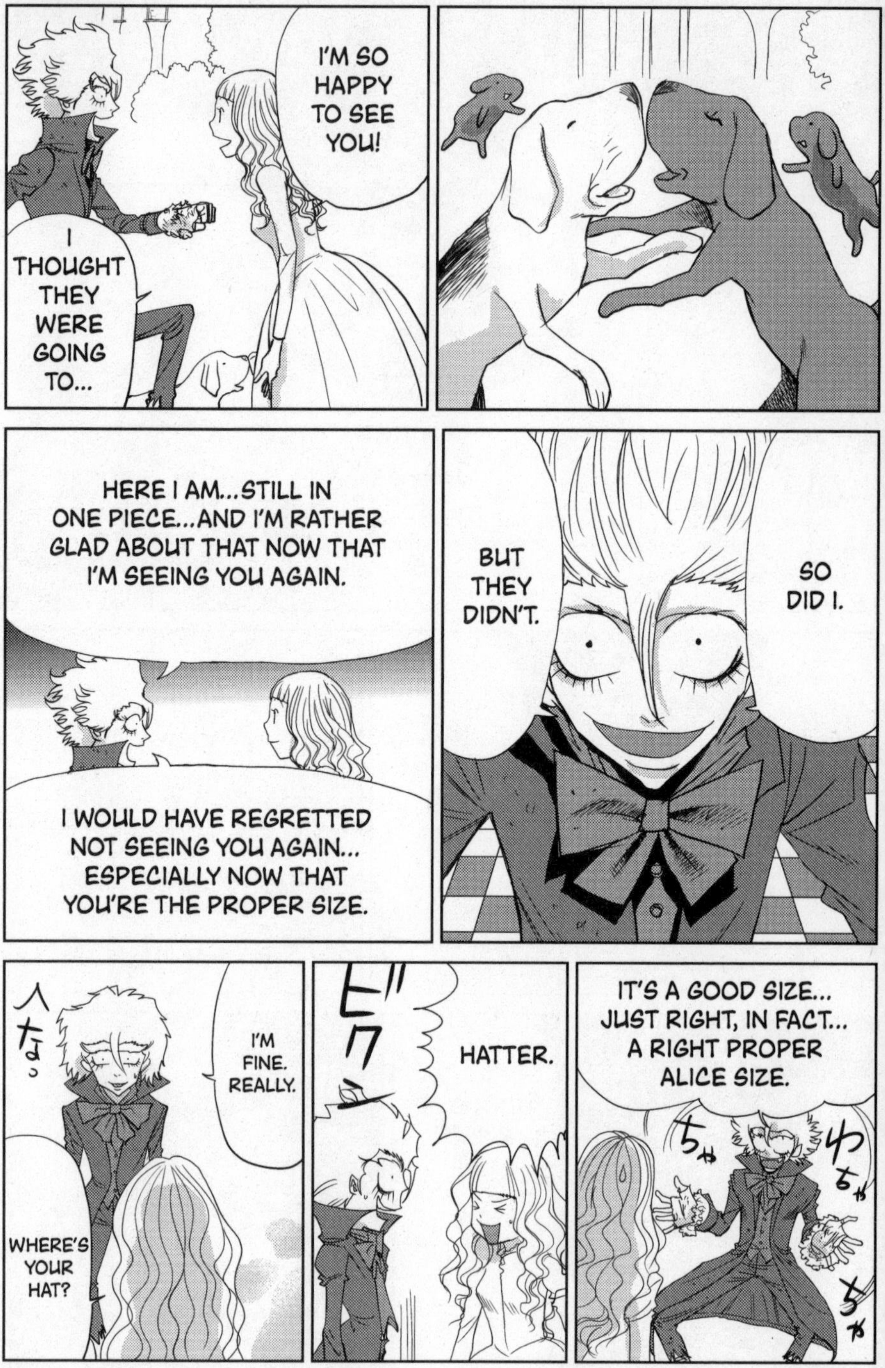

I'M SO HAPPY TO SEE YOU!
I THOUGHT THEY WERE GOING TO...
SO DID I.
BUT THEY DIDN'T.
HERE I AM...STILL IN ONE PIECE...AND I'M RATHER GLAD ABOUT THAT NOW THAT I'M SEEING YOU AGAIN.
I WOULD HAVE REGRETTED NOT SEEING YOU AGAIN... ESPECIALLY NOW THAT YOU'RE THE PROPER SIZE.
IT'S A GOOD SIZE... JUST RIGHT, IN FACT... A RIGHT PROPER ALICE SIZE.
わちゃ
ちゃ
HATTER.
ビクン
I'M FINE. REALLY.
へなっ
WHERE'S YOUR HAT?

ぬっ
CHESSUR?
HEY, LOVE ...
... HOW'S THE ARM?
ALL HEALED.
GOODBYE, SWEET HAT.

WHY IS A RAVEN LIKE A WRITING DESK?
A RIDDLE! THIS WILL BE FUN. LET ME THINK ABOUT IT...
YOU DO KNOW WHAT TOMORROW IS.
THE FRABJOUS DAY.
HOW COULD I FORGET? OH, I WISH I'D WAKE UP!

YOU STILL THINK THIS IS A DREAM?
WELL, IT CAN'T POSSIBLY BE REAL. THIS HAS ALL COME FROM MY OWN MIND.
WHICH WOULD MEAN THAT I'M NOT REAL.
NO, I'M SORRY TO SAY. YOU'RE JUST A FIGMENT OF MY IMAGINATION.
I WOULD DREAM UP SOMEONE WHO'S HALF-MAD.
BUT YOU'D HAVE TO BE HALF-MAD...
...TO DREAM ME UP.
I MUST BE, THEN.

I GIVE UP. WHY IS A RAVEN LIKE A WRITING DESK?
I HAVEN'T THE SLIGHTEST IDEA.
I'LL MISS YOU WHEN I WAKE UP.
WHO WILL STEP FORTH TO BE CHAMPION FOR THE WHITE QUEEN?

YOU HAVE VERY POOR EVAPORATING SKILLS. I SHOULD BE THE ONE.
NO, ME!
NO, ME!
THAT WOULD BE I!
IF IT AIN'T ALICE, HE AIN'T DEAD.
NO OTHER SLAYER, NOHOW.

ALICE, YOU CANNOT LIVE YOUR LIFE TO PLEASE OTHERS. THE CHOICE MUST BE YOURS.
BECAUSE WHEN YOU STEP OUT TO FACE THAT CREATURE, YOU WILL STEP OUT ALONE.
ALICE!!

READ THIS WAY

NOTHING WAS EVER ACCOMPLISHED WITH TEARS.
ABSOLEM?
UP HERE, ON THE LEAF.
WHY ARE YOU UPSIDE DOWN?
I'VE COME TO THE END OF THIS LIFE.
YOU'RE GOING TO DIE?
NO. TRANSFORM.

DON'T GO! I NEED YOUR HELP!
I DON'T KNOW WHAT TO DO!
SUCH A STUPID GIRL...
I CAN'T HELP YOU IF YOU DON'T EVEN KNOW WHO YOU ARE.
I'M NOT STUPID! MY NAME IS ALICE. I LIVE IN LONDON. I HAVE A MOTHER NAMED HELEN AND A SISTER NAMED MARGARET.
MY FATHER WAS CHARLES KINGSLEIGH. HE HAD A VISION THAT STRETCHED HALFWAY AROUND THE WORLD AND NOTHING EVER STOPPED HIM. HE WOULD HAVE LIKED IT HERE.
I'M HIS DAUGHTER.
I'M ALICE KINGSLEIGH!

ALICE, AT LAST!
YOU WERE JUST AS DIM-WITTED THE FIRST TIME YOU WERE HERE.
YOU CALLED IT "WONDERLAND," AS I RECALL.
WONDER-LAND.

IT WASN'T A DREAM AT ALL.
IT WAS A MEMORY! THIS PLACE IS REAL!
AND SO ARE YOU.
AND SO IS THE HATTER.
AND THE JABBERWOCKY. REMEMBER, THE VORPAL SWORD KNOWS WHAT IT WANTS.

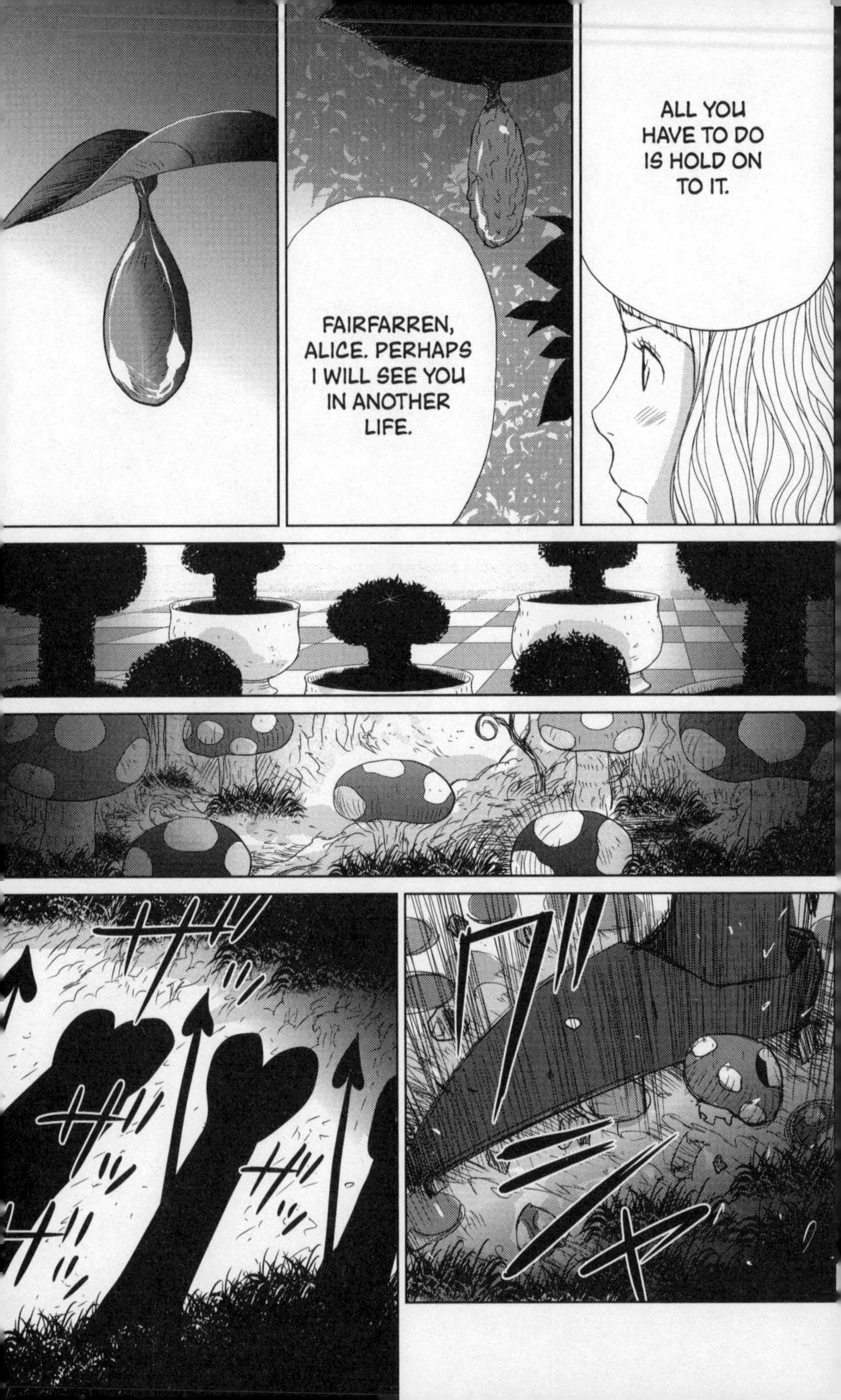
ALL YOU HAVE TO DO IS HOLD ON TO IT.
FAIRFARREN, ALICE. PERHAPS I WILL SEE YOU IN ANOTHER LIFE.

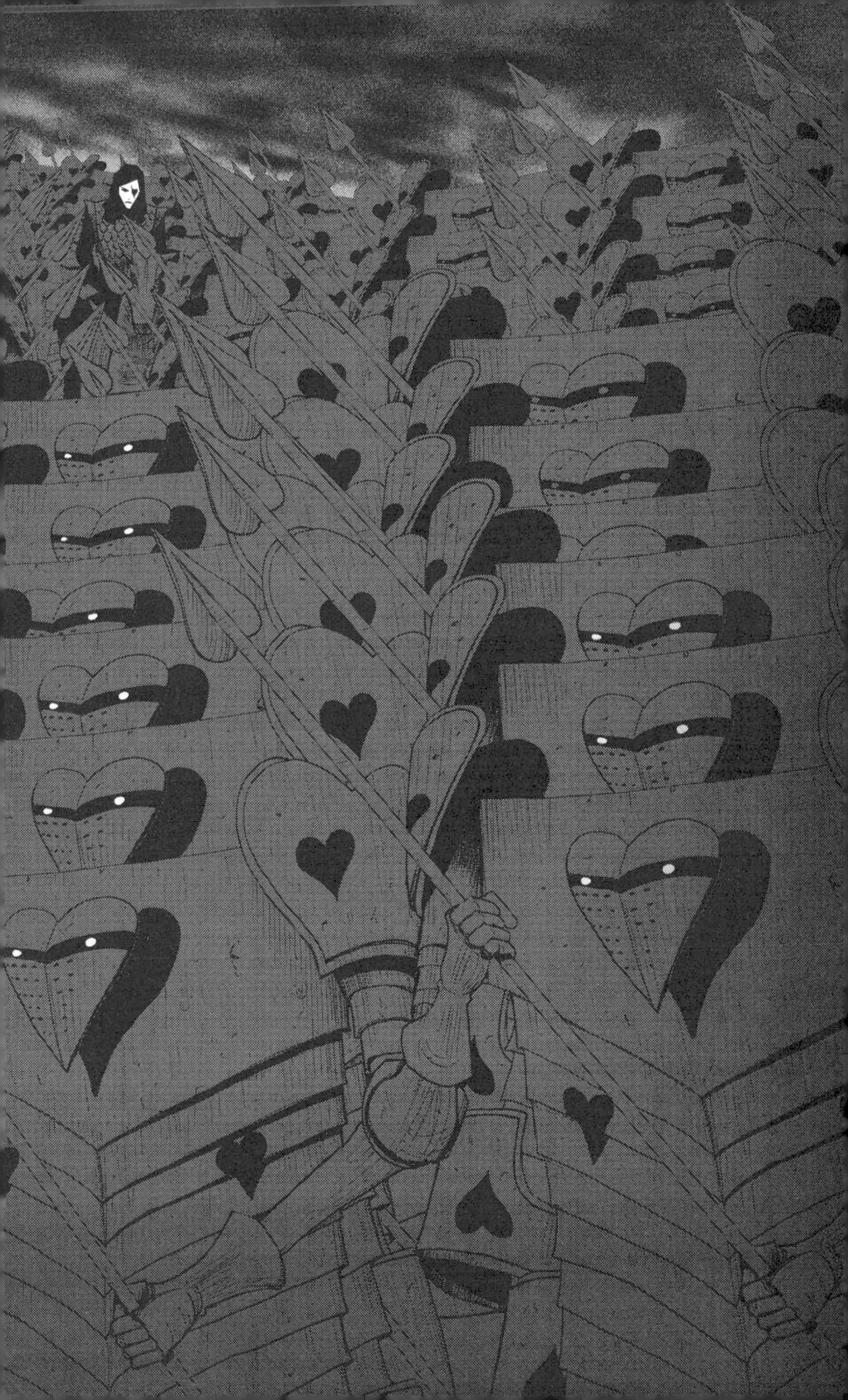

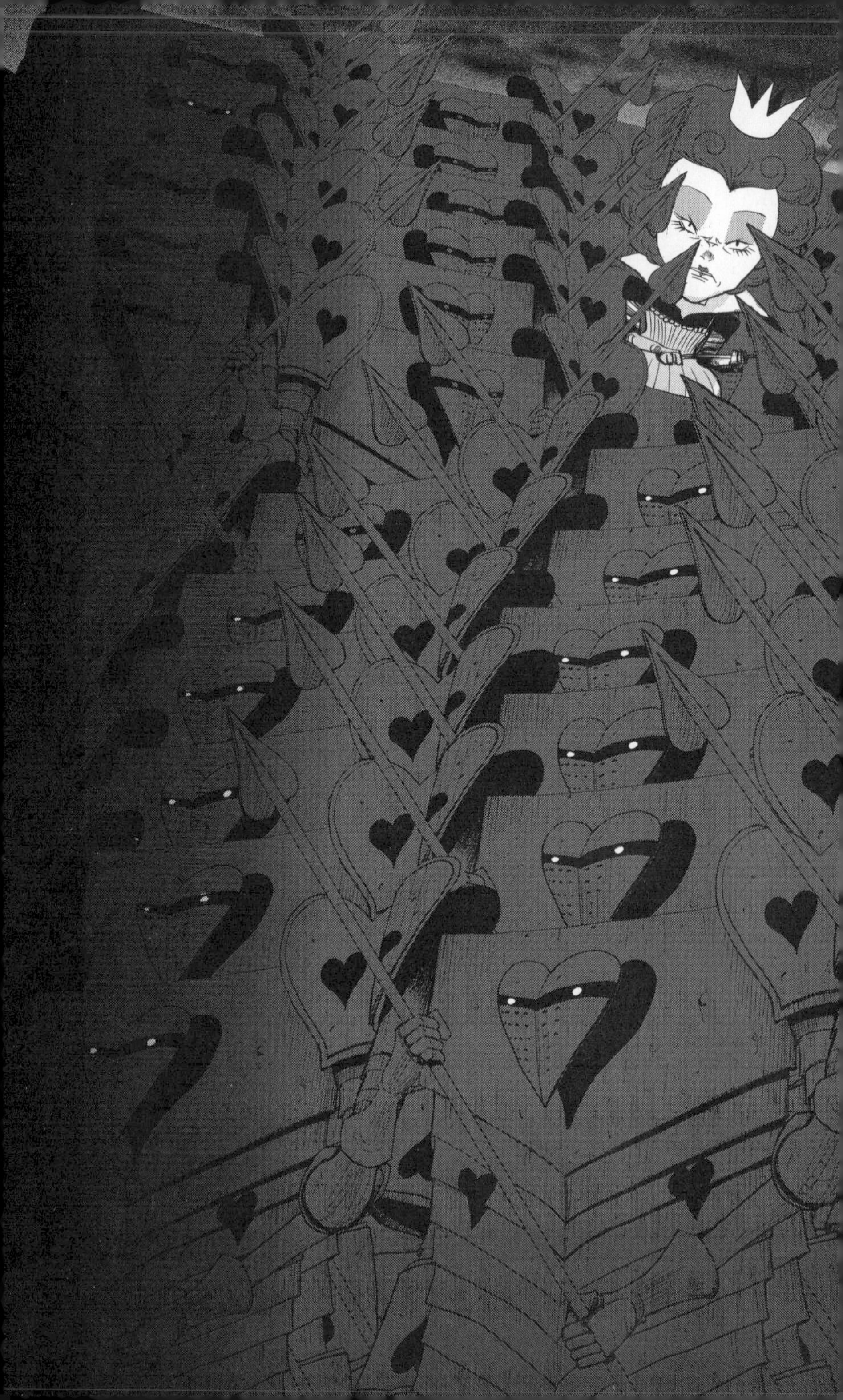

IT'S COMING! LOOK UP!
TO THE TULGEY WOOD!

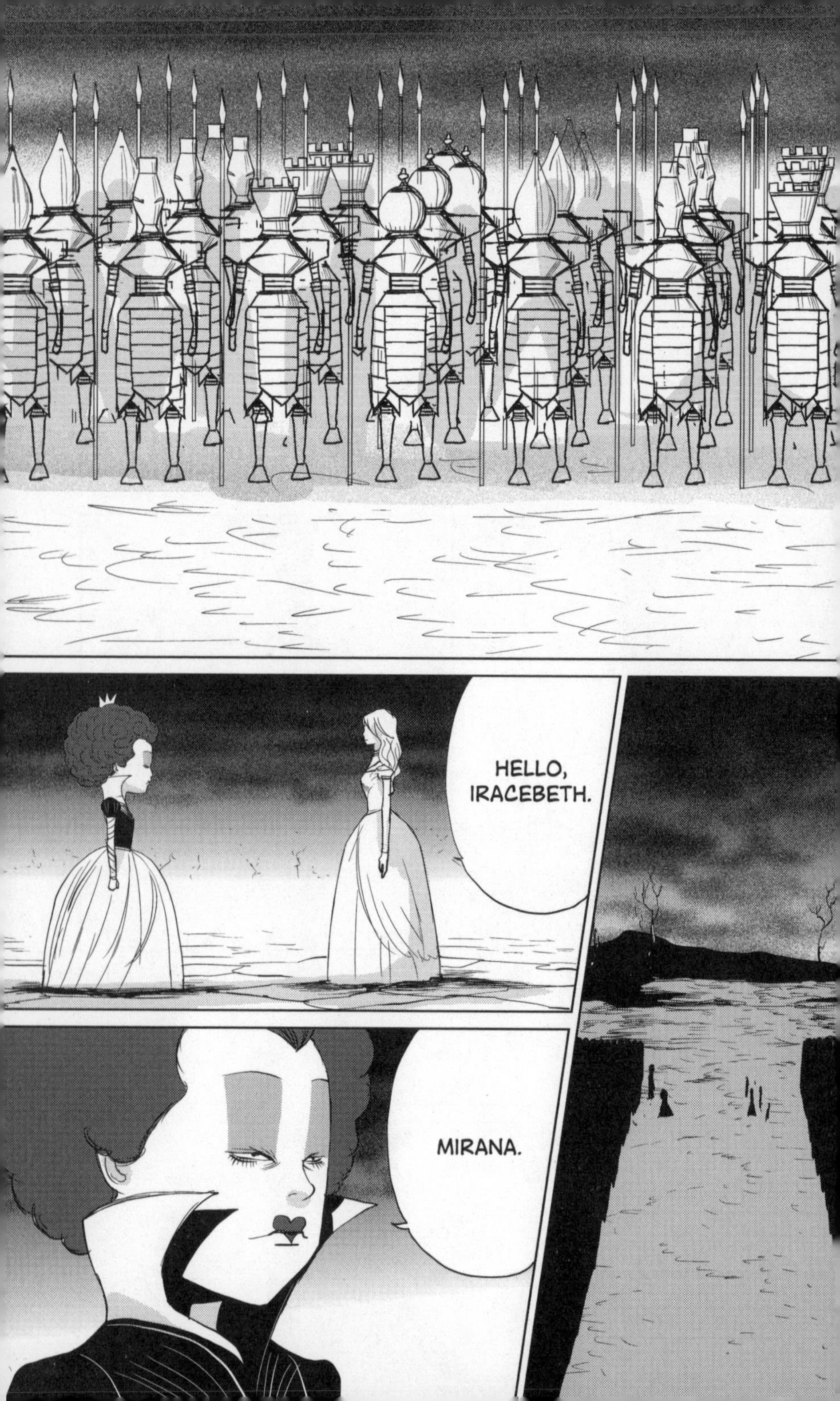
HELLO, IRACEBETH.
MIRANA.

ON THIS THE FRABJOUS DAY, THE QUEENS, RED AND WHITE, SHALL SEND FORTH THEIR CHAMPIONS TO DO BATTLE ON THEIR BEHALF.
HEY, 'RACIE!
OH, 'RACIE ...
WE DON'T HAVE TO FIGHT.
I KNOW WHAT YOU'RE DOING.
YOU THINK YOU CAN BLINK THOSE PRETTY LITTLE EYES AND I'LL MELT LIKE MUMS AND DADDY DID.

JUST GIVE ME MY CROWN.
IT'S MY CROWN!
JABBER-WOCKY!!

ONLY IF YOU BELIEVE IT IS.
BUT THIS IS IMPOS-SIBLE.
"SOMETIMES I BELIEVE AS MANY AS SIX IMPOSSIBLE THINGS BEFORE BREAKFAST."
AN EXCELLENT PRACTICE, BUT AT THE MOMENT, YOU SHOULD JUST FOCUS ON THE JABBERWOCKY.
WHERE IS YOUR CHAMPION, LITTLE SISTER?
HERE.

SIX IMPOSSIBLE THINGS. COUNT THEM.
ONE! THERE'S A POTION THAT CAN MAKE YOU SHRINK.
TWO! AND A CAKE THAT CAN MAKE YOU GROW.
SO, MY OLD FOE, WE MEET ON THE BATTLE-FIELD ONCE AGAIN.
WE HAVE NEVER MET.
NOT YOU, IN-SIGNIFICANT BEARER!!

MY ANCIENT ENEMY, THE VORPAL ONE.

THAT'S ENOUGH CHATTER.

THREE! ANIMALS CAN TALK.

CATS CAN DISAPPEAR.
WATCH YOUR HEAD!
FOUR... FOUR, ALICE!
FIVE! THERE IS A PLACE CALLED WONDERLAND.

SIX...

AND I CAN SLAY THE JABBER-WOCKY!
GRAAAAWGH!

BEHIND YOU!
I CAN MANAGE. THANK YOU.
THE HATTER'S INTERFERING!
OFF WITH HIS HEAD!!

Disney

Alice in Wonderland

11 Anchors Aweigh

キン
ニヤッ

パッ
パッ
パッ
ガバァァ
ポイ
ポイ
ゴゴゴゴ

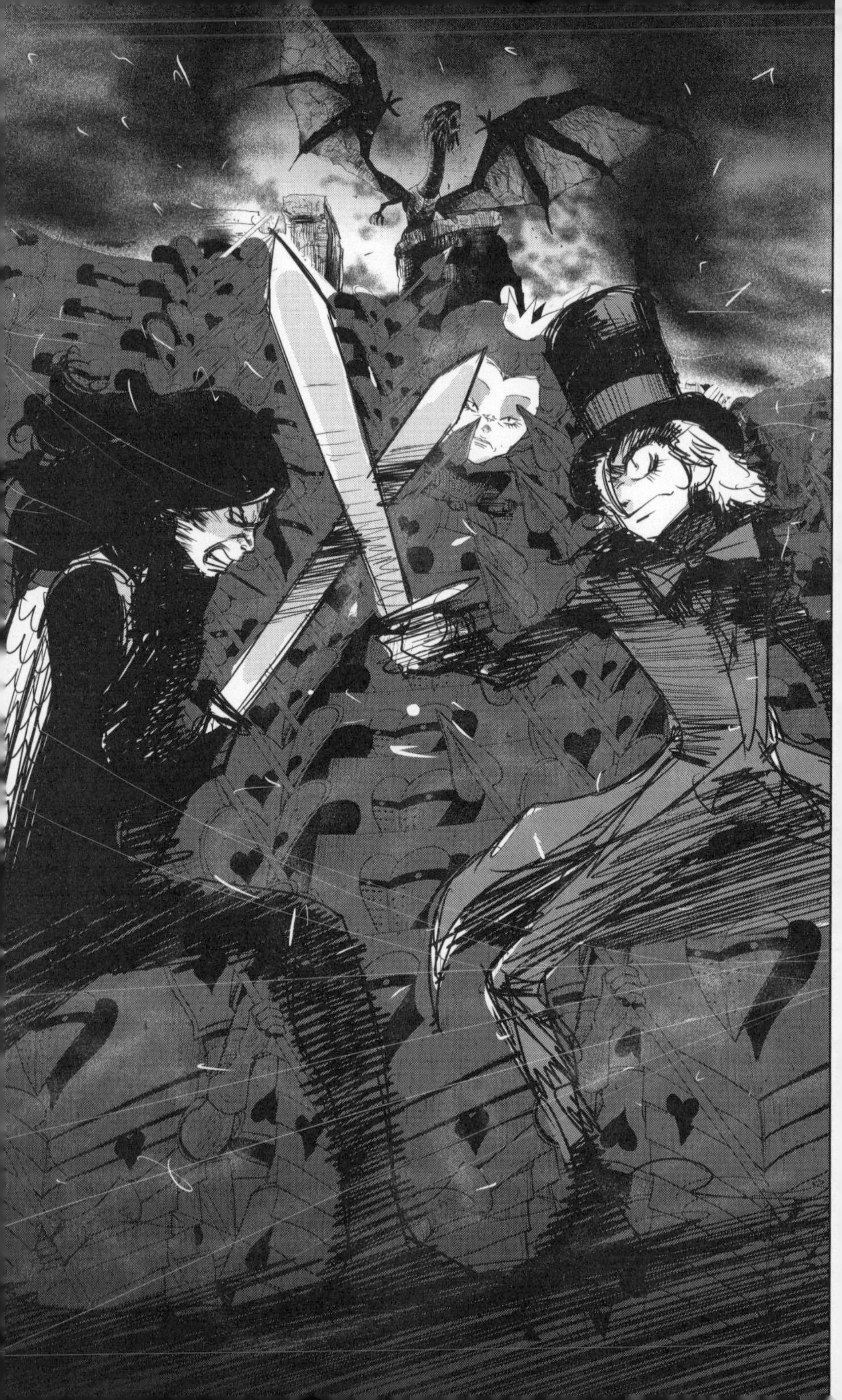

ガッ
ミュッ
ズオオオー

OFF WITH YOUR HEAD!

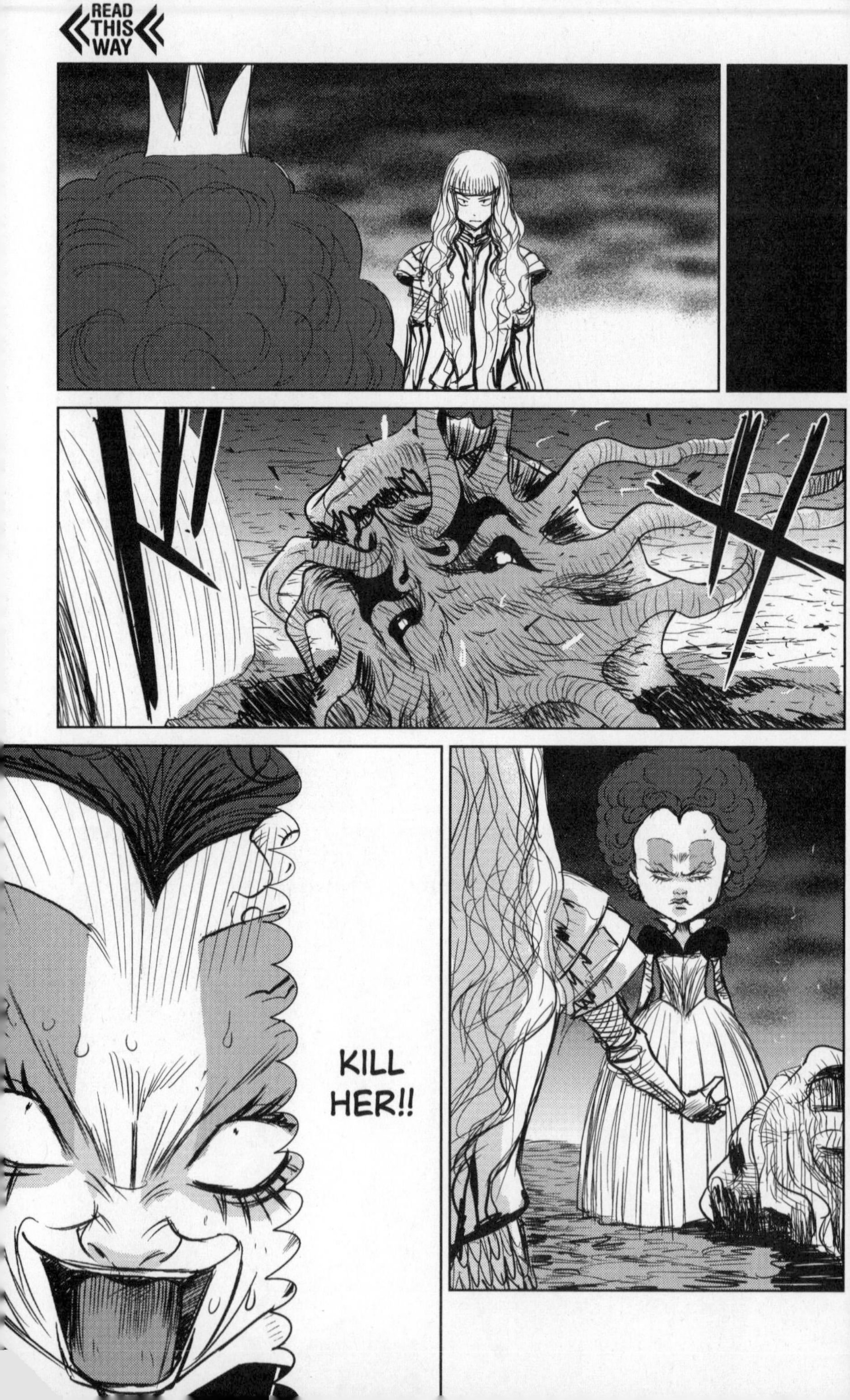
READ THIS WAY
KILL HER!!

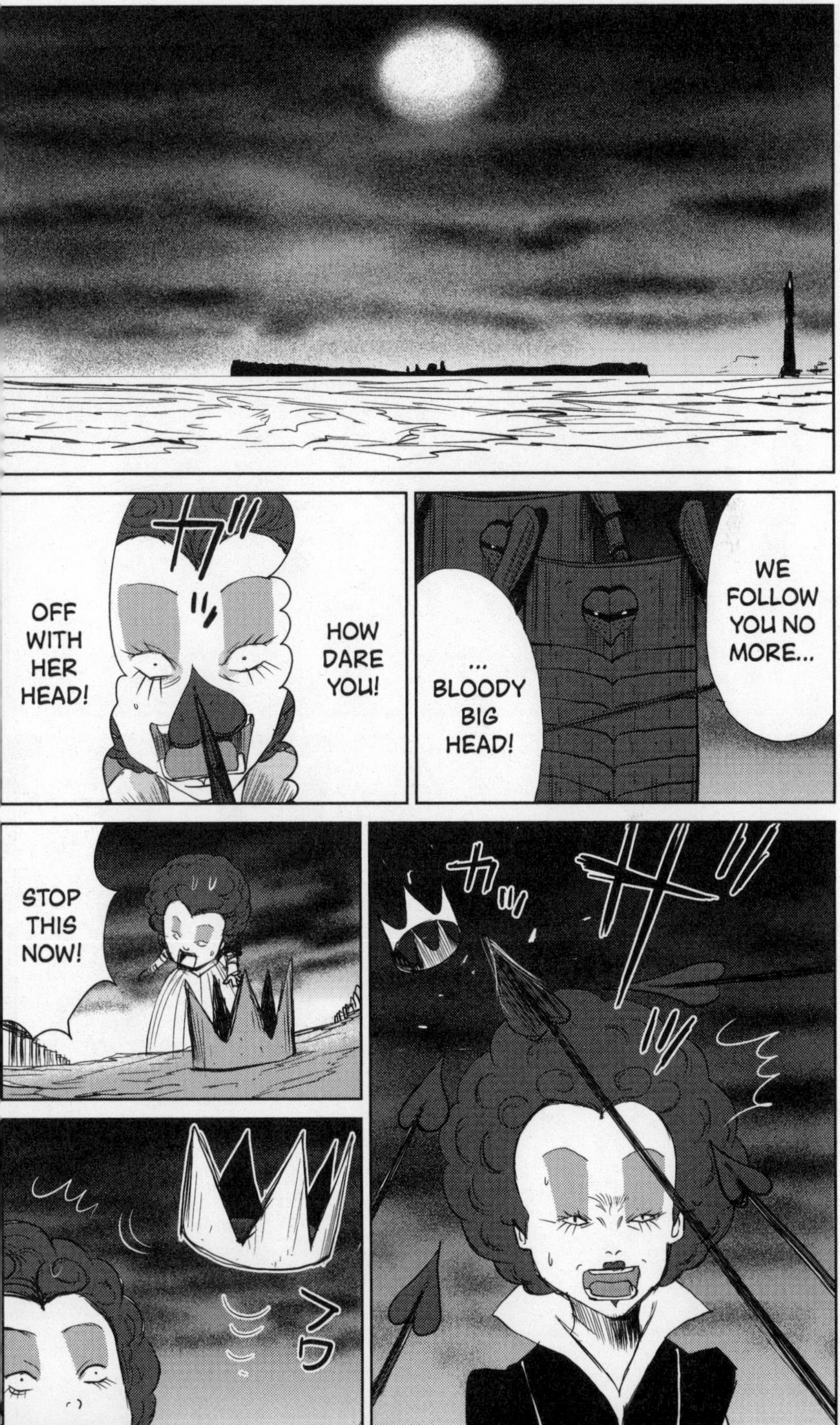
WE FOLLOW YOU NO MORE...
... BLOODY BIG HEAD!
HOW DARE YOU!
OFF WITH HER HEAD!
STOP THIS NOW!

フワフワ
ポン
ボワン
IRACEBETH OF CRIMS, YOUR CRIMES AGAINST UNDERLAND ARE WORTHY OF DEATH. BUT THAT IS AGAINST MY VOWS. THEREFORE, YOU ARE BANISHED TO THE OUTLANDS.
NO ONE IS TO SHOW YOU ANY KINDNESS OR EVER SPEAK A WORD TO YOU. YOU WILL HAVE NOT A FRIEND IN THE WORLD.

MAJESTY, I HOPE YOU BEAR ME NO ILL WILL.
EXCEPT THIS ONE. ILOSOVIC STAYNE, YOU WILL JOIN IRACEBETH IN BANISHMENT FROM THIS DAY UNTIL THE END OF UNDERLAND.
WATCH IT!
AT LEAST WE HAVE EACH OTHER.

KILL ME... PLEASE.
BUT I DO NOT OWE YOU A KINDNESS.
...
ヤッホー
YOU TRIED TO KILL ME!
YOU TRIED TO KILL ME!
スタン
タン
WHAT IS HE DOING?
タン
スタン
タン
OH, FRABJOUS DAY!!
CALLOU! CALLAY!

FUTTER-
WACKEN
...

ポン
がっくし
ポタ

...FOR ALL YOUR EFFORTS ON OUR BEHALF.
...AND BLOOD OF THE JABBERWOCKY. YOU HAVE OUR EVERLASTING GRATITUDE. THIS IS FOR YOU...
WILL THIS TAKE ME HOME?
IF THAT IS WHAT YOU CHOOSE.

READ THIS WAY
YOU COULD STAY.
WHAT AN IDEA... A CRAZY, MAD, WONDERFUL IDEA.

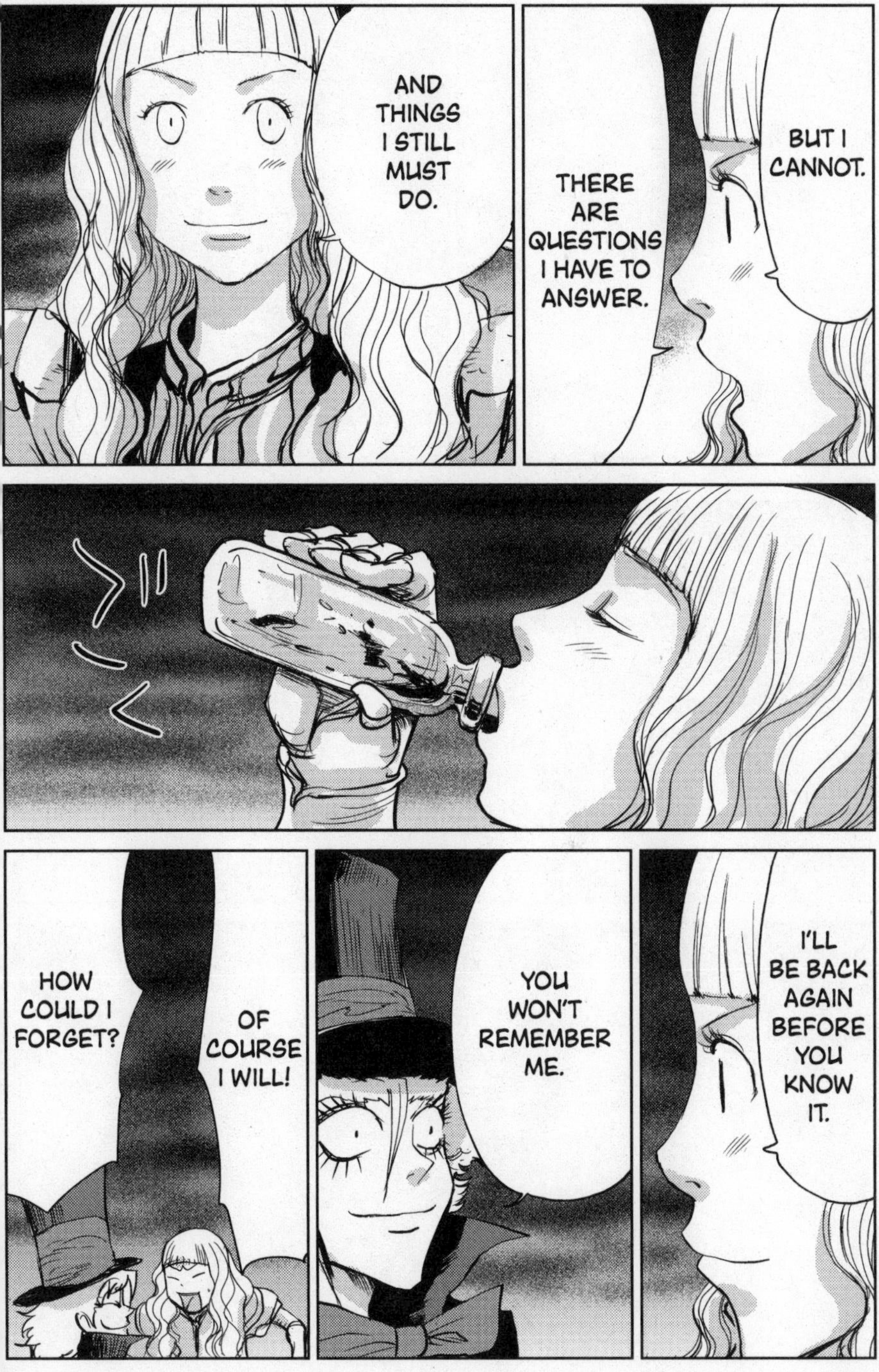
BUT I CANNOT.
THERE ARE QUESTIONS I HAVE TO ANSWER.
AND THINGS I STILL MUST DO.
I'LL BE BACK AGAIN BEFORE YOU KNOW IT.
YOU WON'T REMEMBER ME.
OF COURSE I WILL!
HOW COULD I FORGET?

READ THIS WAY

ひそ ひそ
FAIRFARREN, ALICE...

READ THIS WAY
...MUST HAVE FALLEN IN.

A CASE OF THE NERVES, NO DOUBT.
SHE LEFT ME STANDING THERE WITHOUT AN ANSWER.
ALICE?!
GOOD LORD! ARE YOU ALL RIGHT?

READ THIS WAY

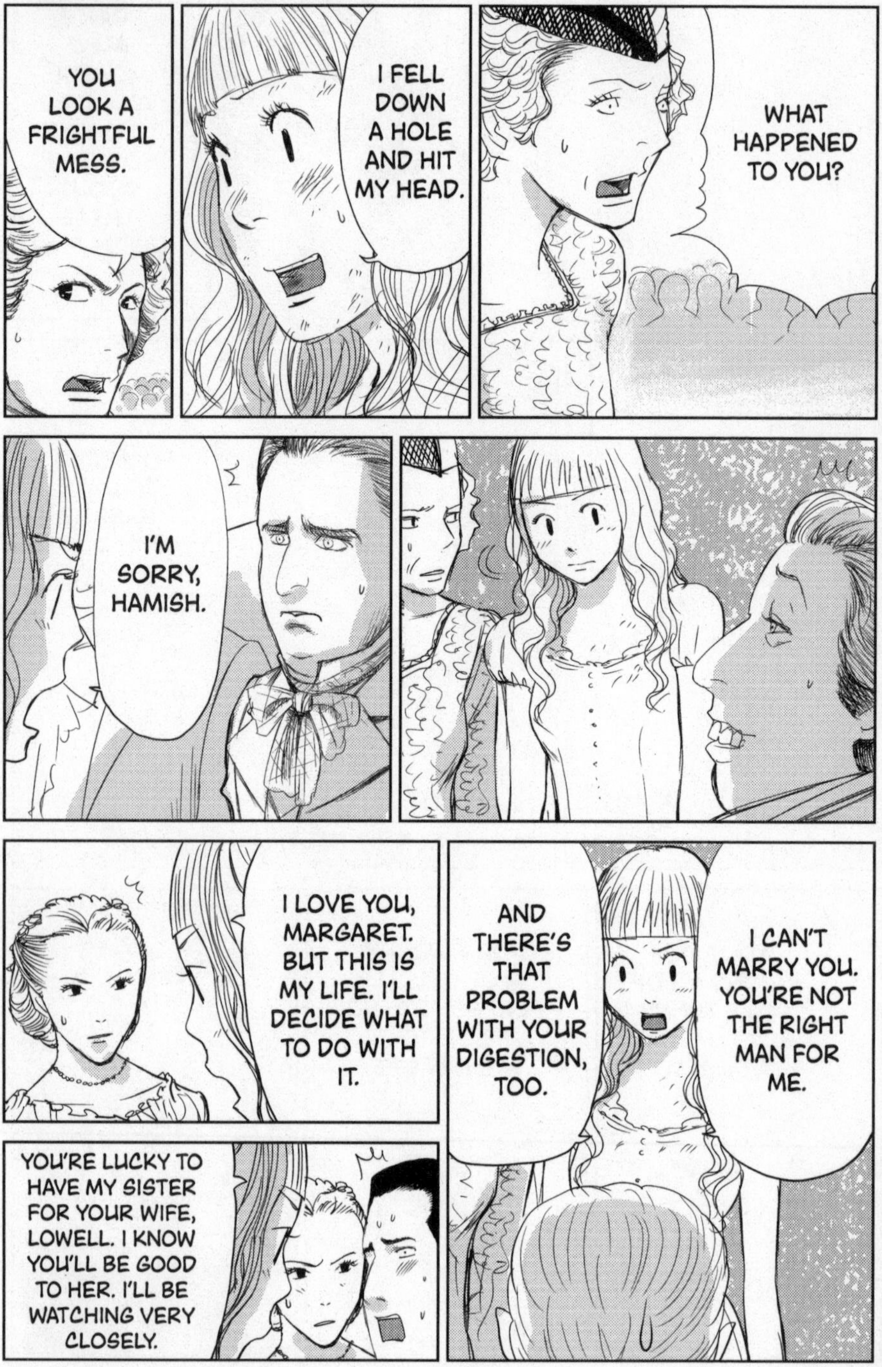
WHAT HAPPENED TO YOU?
I FELL DOWN A HOLE AND HIT MY HEAD.
YOU LOOK A FRIGHTFUL MESS.
I'M SORRY, HAMISH.
I CAN'T MARRY YOU. YOU'RE NOT THE RIGHT MAN FOR ME.
AND THERE'S THAT PROBLEM WITH YOUR DIGESTION, TOO.
I LOVE YOU, MARGARET. BUT THIS IS MY LIFE. I'LL DECIDE WHAT TO DO WITH IT.
YOU'RE LUCKY TO HAVE MY SISTER FOR YOUR WIFE, LOWELL. I KNOW YOU'LL BE GOOD TO HER. I'LL BE WATCHING VERY CLOSELY.

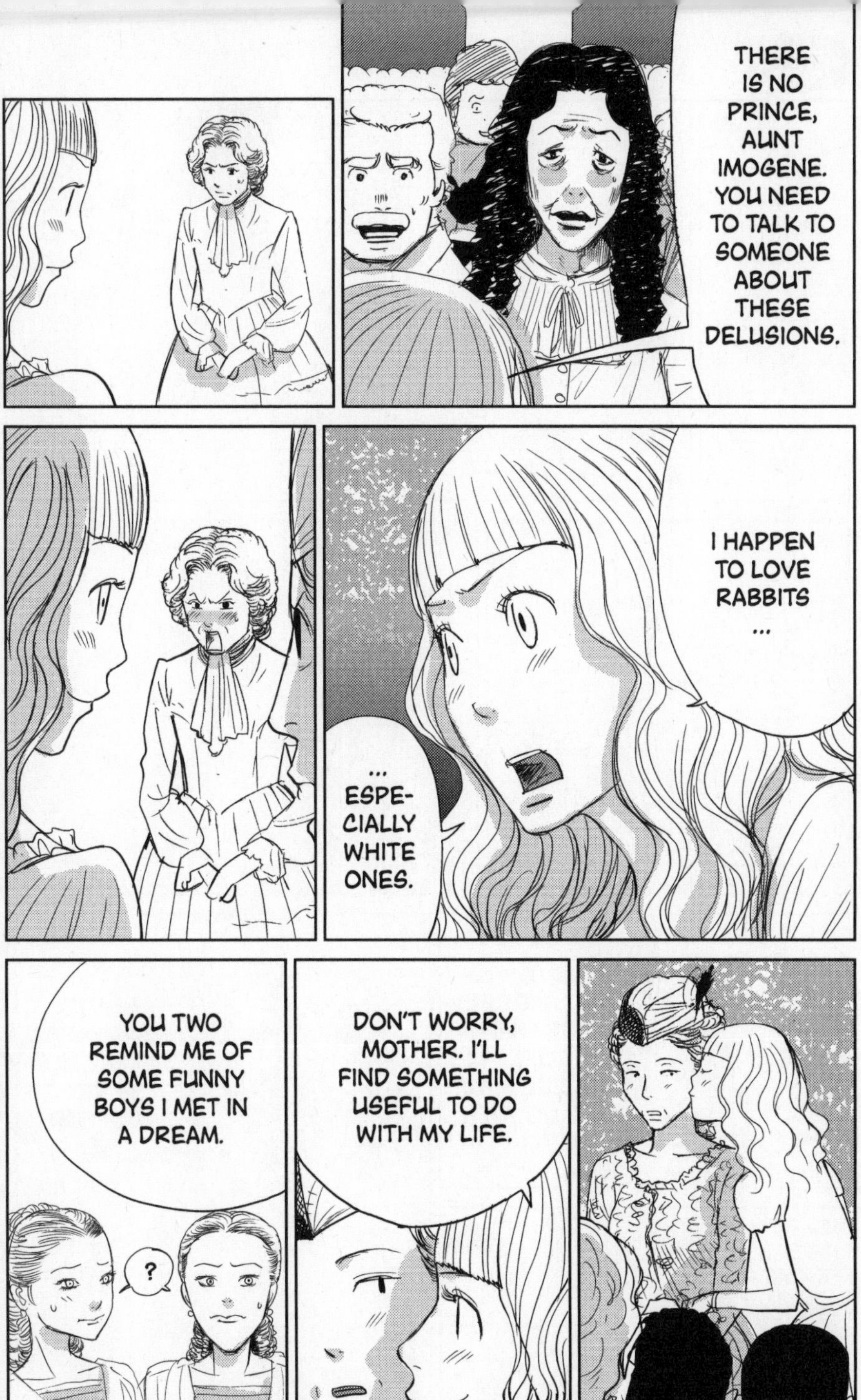
THERE IS NO PRINCE, AUNT IMOGENE. YOU NEED TO TALK TO SOMEONE ABOUT THESE DELUSIONS.
I HAPPEN TO LOVE RABBITS ...
... ESPECIALLY WHITE ONES.
YOU TWO REMIND ME OF SOME FUNNY BOYS I MET IN A DREAM.
?
DON'T WORRY, MOTHER. I'LL FIND SOMETHING USEFUL TO DO WITH MY LIFE.

READ THIS WAY
ANYONE ELSE?
YOU'VE LEFT ME OUT.
NO, I HAVEN'T, SIR. YOU AND I HAVE BUSINESS TO DISCUSS.
THE IMPERTINENCE ...!
I'D LIKE TO HEAR WHAT SHE HAS TO SAY. SHALL WE SPEAK IN THE STUDY?
OH, AND ONE MORE THING...

WHY NOT GO ALL THE WAY TO CHINA? IT'S VAST, THE CULTURE IS RICH, AND WE HAVE A FOOTHOLD IN HONG KONG. TO BE THE FIRST TO TRADE WITH CHINA... CAN YOU IMAGINE IT?
NOT FAR ENOUGH?
MY FATHER TOLD ME HE PLANNED TO EXPAND HIS TRADE ROUTE TO SUMATRA AND BORNEO. BUT I DON'T THINK HE WAS LOOKING FAR ENOUGH.
SINCE YOU'RE NOT GOING TO BE MY DAUGHTER-IN-LAW, PERHAPS YOU WOULD CONSIDER AN APPRENTICESHIP WITH THE COMPANY?
IF YOU WERE ANYONE ELSE, I WOULD SAY YOU'VE LOST YOUR SENSES. BUT I'VE SEEN THAT LOOK BEFORE.

I'D LOVE TO!
SIX MONTHS LATER...

HELLO, ABSOLEM.

Disney
Alice in Wonderland

TOKYOPOP®

Disney

Alice in Wonderland

A

ALICE KINGSLEIGH

Disney

Alice in Wonderland

Concept Artwork

ALICE KINGSLEIGH

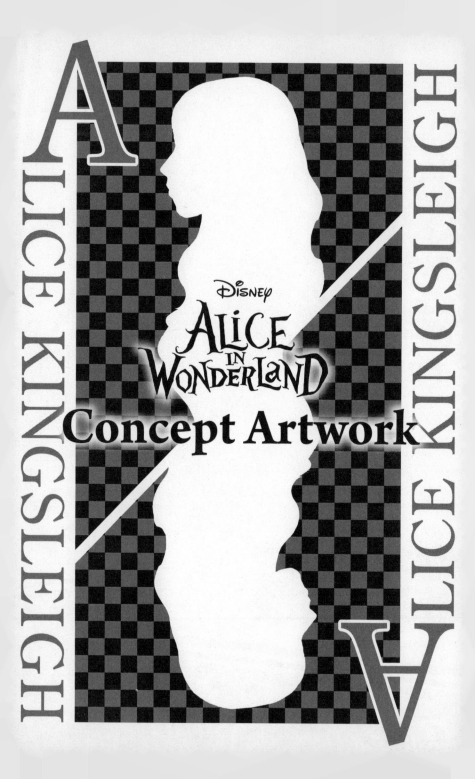

A

アリス・キングスレー
Alice Kingsleigh

Characters of Wonderland

赤の女王
The Red Queen

Characters of Wonderland

帽子屋（マッドハッター）
The Mad Hatter

イロソビック・ステイン
（ハートのジャック）
ILOSOVIC STAYNE
(KNAVE OF HEARTS)

チェシャ猫
CHESHIRE

Characters of Wonderland

トウィードルダム、トウィードルディー
TWEEDLEDEE AND TWEEDLEDUM
白の女王
WHITE QUEEN
アブソレム
ABSOLEM

Disney
Alice in Wonderland

Disney Alice in Wonderland: Special Collector's Manga

By Jun Abe

Retouch and Lettering	- Vibrraant Publishing Studio
Copy Editor	- Julie Taylor
Graphic Designer	- Vibrraant Publishing Studio
Translator	- Jason Muell
Social Media	- Michelle Klein-Hass
Marketing	- Kristen Olson
Editor	- Julie Taylor
Editor-in-Chief & Publisher	- Stu Levy

A TOKYOPOP® Manga

TOKYOPOP and are trademarks or registered trademarks of TOKYOPOP Inc.

TOKYOPOP Inc.
9420 Reseda Blvd Suite 555
Northridge, CA 91324

E-mail: info@TOKYOPOP.com
Come visit us online at www.TOKYOPOP.com

www.facebook.com/TOKYOPOP
www.twitter.com/TOKYOPOP
www.youtube.com/TOKYOPOPTV
www.pinterest.com/TOKYOPOP
www.instagram.com/TOKYOPOP
TOKYOPOP.tumblr.com

ISBN: 978-1-4278-5656-2

First TOKYOPOP printing: May 2016

10 9 8 7 6 5 4 3 2 1

Printed in the USA

STOP!

This is the last page of the book!
You don't want to spoil the fun
and start with the end, do you?

In Japan, *manga* is created in accordance with the native language, which reads right-to-left when vertical. So, in order to stay true to the original, pretend you're in Japan -- just flip this book over and you're good to go!

Here's how:

1
2
3
4
5
6
7
8
9
10

If you're new to *manga*, don't worry, it's easy! Just start at the top right panel and read down and to the left, like in the picture here. Have fun and enjoy authentic *manga* from TOKYOPOP®!!